model for experiencing victory. Every man should read this book and purchase a copy for the other men in his life."

Robby Gallaty
Pastor, Long Hollow Baptist Church, Hendersonville, TN
Author, *Growing Up* and *The Forgotten Jesus*

"This book will speak to every man's heart! Johnny Hunt is a fellow pastor, friend, and mentor. As a pastor, he has learned from thousands of men over the years through His Timothy Barnabas conferences and his dedication to the kingdom. God will speak to your heart, and you will be blessed!"

Rob Zinn
Pastor, Immanuel Baptist Church, Highland, CA

"Many a man would wish he had read this book when he was young. But it's never too late to learn the value of the lessons my friend Johnny Hunt will bring to the reader. He keeps it candid yet profound in its implications. Applying these truths will save you a nightmare of regrets."

Dr. Ravi Zacharias
Speaker and author

"Out of the park! Yes, Johnny Hunt has told it like it is in this book for men. Now is the time every man needs to choose to face his battles courageously. Therefore, act like a man! Release your past, deal with the present, and move toward the future God has for you."

Dr. Ronnie Floyd
Senior Pastor, Cross Church
President, National Day of Prayer
Past president, Southern Baptist Convention

D0179511

UNSPOKEN

JOHNNY HUNT

HARVEST HOUSE PUBLISHERS
EUGENE, OREGON

PROPERTY OF
LINK LIBRARIES/
VIEW LIBRARY DISTRICT

Unless otherwise indicated, all Scripture quotations are taken from the New King James Version®. Copyright © 1982 by Thomas Nelson, Inc. Used by permission. All rights reserved.

Verses marked NIV are taken from the Holy Bible, New International Version®, NIV®. Copyright © 1973, 1978, 1984, 2011 by Biblica, Inc.® Used by permission. All rights reserved worldwide.

Verses marked ESV are from The ESV® Bible (The Holy Bible, English Standard Version®), copyright © 2001 by Crossway, a publishing ministry of Good News Publishers. Used by permission. All rights reserved.

Cover by Bryce Williamson, Eugene, OR

Cover Image © Marcos Wordley / Shutterstock

UNSPOKEN

Copyright © 2018 Johnny Hunt
Published by Harvest House Publishers
Eugene, Oregon 97408
www.harvesthousepublishers.com

ISBN 978-0-7369-7299-4 (pbk.)
ISBN 980-0-7369-7300-7 (eBook)

Library of Congress Cataloging-in-Publication Data

Names: Hunt, Johnny M., 1952- author.
Title: Unspoken: 8 things men are silent about...and how to overcome them / Johnny Hunt.
Description: Eugene, Oregon : Harvest House Publishers, 2018.
Identifiers: LCCN 2017039038 (print) | LCCN 2017048705 (ebook) | ISBN 9780736973007 (ebook) | ISBN 9780736972994 (pbk.)
Subjects: LCSH: Christian men—Religious life.
Classification: LCC BV4528.2 (ebook) | LCC BV4528.2 .H865 2018 (print) | DDC 248.8/42—dc23
LC record available at https://lccn.loc.gov/2017039038

All rights reserved. No part of this publication may be reproduced, stored in a retrieval system, or transmitted in any form or by any means—electronic, mechanical, digital, photocopy, recording, or any other—except for brief quotations in printed reviews, without the prior permission of the publisher.

Printed in the United States of America

17 18 19 20 21 22 23 24 25 26 / VP-SK / 10 9 8 7 6 5 4 3 2 1

To my wife, Janet Lee Allen Hunt. She is not just my soul mate and my companion, but my best friend. No one has had to forgive me so much, and no one has ever loved me so deeply.

NO LONGER PROPERTY OF
ANYTHINK LIBRARIES/
RANGEVIEW LIBRARY DISTRICT

CONTENTS

FOREWORD

"We do not lose heart; though our outer man is decaying,
yet our inner man is being renewed day by day"
(2 Corinthians 4:16).

What a powerful exhortation from Paul: Everything that the world observes about us and uses to define us will fritter away with time. But that which is on the inside—our faith, our grit, our determination, our perseverance, our convictions, our spirit—the Lord renews that each day as a means to make us a better man, a better husband, a better father and grandfather, a better representative of Christ.

In his new book *Unspoken*, my dear friend and former pastor Johnny Hunt tackles this concept head-on, using the power of the Word combined with his own unique life experiences to bring clarity to the difficult and unique issues with which men struggle.

In his own plainspoken clear voice, Johnny speaks directly and without judgment to things we often bottle up or avoid...emotions and doubts that we think make us weak, incapable, unworthy, or even less of a man. And if we sweep them under the rug without any resolution, they only fester into bigger problems with bigger consequences. We hurt ourselves, and by extension, we hurt our families, our friends, our work, our ministries.

These challenges are real, and they often prevent us from living in the fullness of God's plan for us. Johnny not only addresses these problems and their root causes, but he teaches and encourages us that there is a better way, that God provides a path to overcome whatever struggles we may have.

Johnny puts his finger directly on one of the most important truths of our spiritual journey: Among the most meaningful tools that God gives us is friendships with other Christian men, those with whom we can talk openly and earnestly. We need one another. With one another, just like Mark wrote about Jesus, we grow in wisdom and stature, and in favor with God and man.

Inner struggles are part of the human condition. How we deal with them, though, defines us. Any man who wants to tackle what is ahead of him within the confines of God's plan should read this book. Thank you, Johnny, for giving us a blueprint in plain English.

May God speak to you through the words on these pages and richly bless your life.

Sonny Perdue
Former Governor of Georgia and
US Secretary of Agriculture

BECOMING THE MEN GOD MADE US TO BE

D eep within the recesses of the heart of every man beats the strong desire to be the person God created him to be. At the same time, every man is like the moon: We all have our hidden side.

Long ago I lost count of the number of emails and letters I have received from wives concerned about their husbands. These concerned spouses knew their men were struggling, but could not get them to open up and speak with anyone about it.

In my mind, I can still see the note. A wife had written to express her appreciation to me for encouraging her husband to start sharing his deepest secrets. Did it hurt her to learn of those secrets? Of course it did. But something about his vulnerability and transparency drew her to him. Even in the midst of her pain and hurt, she was able to accept her husband for who he was at that moment in his life's journey, and then join with him to help him and watch him become more than a conqueror.

I pray that God would use this book in your life to be a source of encouragement for you to find a few individuals with whom you can feel safe enough to talk openly about your struggles. I pray that you will find a small, faithful group of men who will become committed to each other and help one another get back up when one of you falls. You don't need to stay knocked down permanently in the areas where you desire to be your utmost for His highest!

God has indeed made powerful resources available for us—resources that enable us to walk in victory. Every one of us, regardless of our background or past, can know a life of love and obedience that leads to abiding peace and joy. Deep inside, isn't that what you desire? I know it's what I want!

WHAT'S AHEAD

I've divided this book into three parts. The first part, "What Keeps Us Silent," looks into some of the main reasons we keep our mouths closed about crucial issues that the Lord would have us talk over with one another. Some of these reasons have to do with culture and biology, while others have more to do with the "hidden side" of men mentioned earlier.

Part 2, "Where Silence Is Killing Us," delves into eight of the most critical issues that men commonly refuse to discuss. I try to understand why this silence is killing us, and how we can move into a healthier, new trajectory for ourselves that will land us in a much better spot.

Part 3, "A Place to Untie Our Tongues," encourages every Christian man to seek out other believing men so that together we can strengthen, encourage, and embolden each other to live in a way that blesses those around us and honors and glorifies God. We were made for this! And we will not find the satisfaction in life or the thrill of living that God wants for us until we unloose our tongues in the company of faithful men. Together, let's become the men, the husbands, the fathers, the leaders that God made us to be.

MY PRAYER FOR YOU

As you go chapter by chapter through this book, I pray that the truth you read will unfold in powerful ways that will give you a deeper revelation into who you are and who you can be. I have no interest in writing a self-help book. What I hope to do, more than anything else, is to help you see and appropriate the grace that is available to you in Jesus, and to focus on the hope that He holds out to you, even now. I pray that you would read, be encouraged, and then pass it along.

Pastor Johnny

PART 1:

WHAT KEEPS US SILENT

THE SILENCE
OF THE RAMS

We met at a restaurant. As he sat in the booth with his wife at his side, he got ready to tell me his story. He began by saying that he wished he had spoken with me months before at our annual Southern Baptist Convention.

"I believe that if I had told you then about my struggle," he declared, "and about what my heart was entertaining, you would have thrown me a life preserver."

And then, in a voice filled with both sadness and regret, he described his adulterous relationship with his secretary. His ministry was over, he said, and his heart was broken. No one had to tell me that his marriage was clearly struggling. It looked as though his wife, who remained mostly quiet throughout our meeting, had to exercise every bit of strength just to keep from rushing out of that restaurant.

I listened as this wounded man poured out his pain and remorse—but by then, I couldn't do much to help. Had he spoken to me months before, we might have been able to avoid this whole tear-filled scene. But he'd kept all this hidden deep within.

Why do so many men refuse to speak about the sensitive areas of their lives? It seems that whenever anyone gets too near to an area that feels especially "close to home," many men shut down the conversation in an attempt to keep that area of life private or hidden. That was my friend's problem.

I would love to tell you that his story had a good ending, but I can't. The truth is, he did not offer a totally honest confession that day. I'm sure his tears were real, as was his regret and remorse. He felt truly guilty for what he had done, and he wished he'd never started down that path.

But is that enough? No, it's not, and not by a long shot. In a short time, this sorry-but-unrepentant friend returned to the waiting arms of his former secretary.

LISTEN CAREFULLY, SPEAK HONESTLY

For the last twenty years I have been deeply involved in mentoring young men preparing for ministry. After all these years, I have noted that one of the single greatest traits of successful young pastoral candidates is what I'd call *teachability*. An unteachable spirit and a refusal to take advice from others usually reveals a great deal of pride and arrogance, which almost always signals a flameout in the making.

A big part of teachability includes the desire to listen carefully and to engage in honest dialogue—and really, that commitment has to go both ways. Both the mentor *and* the student need to make a commitment to listen to each other respectfully and to interact with one another honestly. Without that kind of mutual commitment, not much genuine mentoring can take place.

The more I think about it, the more I doubt that *any* man can get very far in his life or in his walk with God if he lacks a teachable spirit. Scripture overflows with exhortations for us to listen, and it frequently urges us to have conversations with one another designed to encourage mutual spiritual growth. Along these lines, James wrote, "So speak and so do as those who will be judged by the law of liberty" (James 2:12).

When we neglect either careful listening or honest speaking, bad things always happen. Love grows cold, and our hearts grow hard. We begin to lose the ability to celebrate the success of others, and bitter conflict erupts. If we're not careful, we lose all spiritual sensitivity and we quickly move into spiritual apathy, which results in all sorts of heartache. So the stakes are high!

Even so, we men often make light of our unwillingness to talk about issues that make us uneasy. We jest about our silence and almost celebrate our refusal to talk. We enjoy telling jokes like these:

- Women like silent men; they actually think they're listening.

- A man had a reputation among his friends as brief and to the point. He seldom said much. One day, a saleswoman selling cosmetics knocked on his door and asked to see his wife. The man told her his wife wasn't home. "Well," she replied, "could I please wait for her?" The man directed her to the kitchen and left her there for more than three hours.

  Eventually the worried saleswoman called out to the man, "May I know where your wife is?"

  "She went to the cemetery," he replied.

  "And when is she returning?"

  "I don't really know," he said. "She's been there eleven years now."

REASONS FOR OUR SILENCE

Not all the reasons for our silence can be traced to sin, as easy as that would be for a pastor to claim and as predictable as you might expect it to be. I can identify at least three sources for our reticence to talk that have little, if anything, to do with a natural male inclination toward evil:

- biology
- father's example
- cultural norms

Let's briefly consider each one in turn.

Biology
Two daughters were born into the family of a friend of mine within nineteen months of each other. Eight years later, my friend and his wife

welcomed a "surprise son" into their home. These parents are learning what countless others have learned before them: Boys are *different* from girls.

Their son, now almost three years old, has a motor that just doesn't stop. Ever. My friend says that his boy is perpetually "five seconds from destruction."

"You literally can't take your eyes off of him for more than five seconds," he says, "or he'll get into something it's not safe for him to get into, take apart something that's supposed to stay together, break something he's not supposed to touch, stack something high that needs to stay by itself on the ground. It's exhausting."

His daughters, by contrast, could play quietly by themselves for long periods without blowing up the kitchen or seeing if the cat liked taking showers. Raising daughters presents different challenges (the teen years loom on the horizon for him) than rearing sons, and because he never thought he'd have a son, he can't say he and his wife were fully prepared for the change. They'd read about the differences and spoken with friends about them, but it's a very different thing to actually experience those unique challenges.

Just a couple decades ago it was fashionable to claim that most behavioral differences between girls and boys were a function of culture and upbringing, not biology. Today the claim is harder to make, since many studies have shown how male and female physiology, from the very beginning, create significant differences in behavior.

In his book *Raising Boys by Design*, Dr. Gregory Jantz describes dozens of key differences between the male and female brains that contribute to significant behavioral differences between the sexes.[1] In fact, researchers have already discovered about one hundred gender differences in the brain, all of which contribute in some way to the distinct ways males and females tend to interact with the world. Scientists have divided these many differences into four general categories: Processing, chemistry, structure, and activity. We can't go into depth here, but I do want you to see how male physiology contributes to the common perception that females talk more (and want to) than do males.

The brains of men and women process thought differently. All brains feature two primary kinds of tissue: "gray matter" that processes specific kinds of information and action requests in highly focalized centers, and "white matter" that provides the brain's networking grid, allowing its various parts to communicate with each other. Can you guess which kind of tissue the brains of most guys tend to use the most? If you guessed gray matter, you win a prize. Male brains tend to utilize nearly *seven* times more gray matter for activity, while female brains tend to utilize nearly *ten* times more white matter. This means that while most guys can readily focus on tasks, often leading to tunnel vision— "Once they are deeply engaged in a task or game, they may not demonstrate much sensitivity to other people or their surroundings," Dr. Jantz writes[2]— females can usually transition more quickly between tasks.

While male and female brains use the same basic neurochemicals, how they use them and to what degree differ. Female brains, for example, use more serotonin, a neurochemical that helps us sit still, and oxytocin, which assists in relationship bonding. Male brains use more testosterone, a chemical that prompts more aggression.

When I think of this physiological difference in connection with my friend's active toddler, I can foresee a likely future trajectory for him. As this boy grows up, he'll have to learn to control his aggression, his tendency to be loud, his impulse to interrupt, to talk over the top of others, and to yell. After years of hearing, "Not so loud!" and "Wait your turn," and "Use your quiet voice, please," he may well be conditioned to think it might just be easier to remain silent. I mean, if he can't talk like he naturally wants to talk, then why talk at all?

Next, the structural differences between the brains of most males and females also lead to differences in the ways they communicate. Because of these differences, females tend to "input or absorb more sensorial and emotive information than males do," which means they "tend to sense a lot more of what is going on around them throughout the day, and they retain that sensorial information more than men."[3] Even before birth,

> females tend to have verbal centers on both sides of the
> brain, while males tend to have verbal centers on only the

left hemisphere. This is a significant difference. Girls tend to use more words when discussing or describing incidence, story, person, object, feeling, or place. Males not only have fewer verbal centers in general but also, often, have less connectivity between their word centers and their memories or feelings. When it comes to discussing feelings and emotions and senses together, girls tend to have an advantage, and they tend to have more interest in talking about these things.[4]

Finally, there's even a physiological reason why females tend to spend more time thinking about emotions than males do (and therefore talking about them). Females usually have more blood flow in their brains because of their greater white matter activity, which prompts them to spend more time recalling items from their emotive memory. Male brains tend to analyze such memories a little, but then move on to the next task.

Biology, then, plays a role in why men often remain silent when they really need to speak up. While biology provides no excuse for refusing to talk when talk is required— "Hey, my genes won't let me"— it does help to explain some of the hurdles we men need to jump in order to become the husbands, fathers, leaders, and men of God our Lord calls us to be.

Father's Example

I was raised by a single mom. My father divorced my mother when I was seven years old. I remember my father's strict discipline, but I don't recall a single conversation I had with him. Never did my father sit me down and explain his discipline or help me to understand why he considered one kind of behavior better than another. I simply did not have a father figure in my life, a man I could use as an example for productively moving forward.

As a result of having no father present in my home, I spent lots of time with my mother. To this day, I generally find it easier to speak to ladies than to men, mostly because of my upbringing. Despite this, long ago I committed to being with men and to sharing openly and honestly with them of my struggles. I've had to work at it, but it's been worth every ounce of extra effort.

A lot of guys have fathers in their lives for much longer than I did, but the example some of these dads left behind doesn't help much. Boys watch as their fathers yell and threaten and bully in order to get their way. They observe as their dads disengage emotionally, walk away from important discussions, and even hop in the car and take off for parts unknown just to avoid talking about subjects they find threatening or distasteful.

Whether we realize it or not, we notice, pick up on, and even mimic behavior we see modeled in front of us. We may not even like the behavior, we may in fact grow to despise it, but the examples we grow up with tend to shape our own actions to one degree or another. If you had a dad who didn't talk much at home, chances are you'll lean toward becoming a man of few words. You'll have to work at overcoming this early training in order to become the man God is calling you to be.

At the age of twenty, when I came to faith in Christ, I was blessed with a heavenly Father. Ever since that day, I have had a lot of catching up to do! I have never wanted to use my misfortune as an excuse for my deficiencies; instead, I have worked to press into Christ as my father. Over the years, I have learned a great deal from Him and His people. Other men have presented me with outstanding, positive role models of what it means to be an effective, loving husband and father. In countless ways, they have taught me that it's not the truth I know, but the truth I obey, that makes the difference.

Cultural Influences

While culture tends to shift and change over time—a time traveler from the 1950s would hardly recognize America today—we still live in a society that largely endorses the "strong, silent type." The Marvel Comics action heroes that have burst from the pages of classic comic books to the 3-D screens of modern Hollywood all tend to wallop the bad guys first and ask questions later. They're long on punching and shooting and short on conversation and debate, unless the conversation includes a lot of snappy put-downs, insults, verbal abuse, and ridicule.

Boys still grow up hearing a lot of sayings that, in essence, tell them, "You ought to leave most of the talking to girls." In one way or another, they're still the targets of messages such as the following:

- Crying is for girls
- Real men don't waste their words
- Man up and shut up
- A real man doesn't call the plumbers

The words of Michel de Montaigne, a sixteenth-century French essayist and skeptic, still resonate with a large portion of contemporary culture: "A good marriage would be between a blind wife and a deaf husband."

To be sure, our culture sends other messages to boys and men besides these; but it remains true that we continue to hear jokes and proverbs and sayings and statements that all declare, in one way or another, "Guys act, women talk."

These kinds of cultural elements that encourage males to clam up or to speak roughly—in some cases, elements that suggest something's wrong with a guy if he actually wants to open up and talk about issues important to his friends or loved ones or God—make it more difficult for followers of Christ to obey biblical commands such as "Let no corrupt word proceed out of your mouth, but what is good for necessary edification, that it may impart grace to the hearers" (Ephesians 4:29). More difficult, yes, but *not* impossible.

One way in which culture can make it difficult for a Christian man to honor God with his life is that it can influence him almost invisibly. Do fish notice water? Probably not, since they never swim in anything but the wet stuff. In a similar way, we "swim" in the cultural context of our day, and often we simply accept it just as naturally as we breathe air.

This helps to explain why we can look throughout history and note periods and eras where the Christians of those days accepted certain things as "normal" that today we would consider wrong and even vile. Slavery comes to mind, as does racial segregation. Less important issues also come to mind. If you've lived a few years, you can probably take out a photo album from a couple decades ago and see yourself clothed in some outfit considered stylish at the time but that today brings guffaws. That's also true about haircuts, cars, beach attire, etc. At the time, who knew? We all swam in that culture and everyone drank the same Kool-Aid, so we hardly noticed.

If we want to become men who make a difference in this world and who want to honor God with our lives, then we *have* to start noticing. We can't leave unspoken the words and conversations and discussions that the Lord says we *must* voice if we are to grow up in Jesus.

The only real question is, Do you want to grow up in Jesus?

AN ANCIENT PROBLEM

I don't want to pretend that men who long to lead godly lives always find it easy to speak up whenever the moment and situation call for it. Even the greatest heroes in Scripture occasionally (or even often) stumbled in this area. I think of great men who earned biblical descriptions such as "the friend of God," "a man after God's own heart," and "the twelve." But each of them, more than once, left things unspoken that they should have said—to their own detriment and to the injury of friends or family.

Abraham, "the friend of God" (James 2:23; see also Isaiah 41:8), put a great many people in danger by refusing to speak up when he most needed to open his mouth. Just before he and his beautiful wife, Sarai, traveled through a pagan country, he persuaded her to tell the king that she was his sister, not his wife. Abraham (then called Abram) feared that if the king wanted Sarai and her beauty for his own, he could simply say to his soldiers, "Kill her husband," and he'd marry the lovely widow. By choosing to keep silent about the truth, however, Abram put in danger not only his wife, but the whole royal court.

God Himself exposed Abram's deceit when He appeared to the king in a dream. "Indeed you are a dead man because of the woman whom you have taken," the Lord said, "for she is a man's wife" (Genesis 20:3).

The frightened king protested, "Lord, will You slay a righteous nation also? Did he not say to me, 'She is my sister'?" The worried man then explained, "In the integrity of my heart and innocence of my hands I have done this" (Genesis 20:4-5).

After Abram received a stinging rebuke, the situation resolved itself peacefully; but had he not left the truth unspoken, no frightening incident would have occurred in the first place. And did I mention that this was the *second* time Abram had pulled this trick? He did it first in Egypt (Genesis 12:11-20).

King David, "a man after [God's] own heart" (1 Samuel 13:14; Acts 13:22), evidently made a habit of not speaking up in his own home. His failure as a responsible father to verbally admonish one of his handsome sons, Adonijah, eventually led to the young man's untimely death. As a prelude to describing how Adonijah died, the Bible says, "His father had not rebuked him at any time by saying, 'Why have you done so?'" (1 Kings 1:6).

Why didn't David rebuke his son "at any time"? Well, he was a busy guy. He had lots of kids. He had court duties to attend to, ambassadors to host, battles to win, soldiers to inspect, generals to instruct, palaces to build, trips to take, negotiations to lead, ceremonies to conduct. He probably left the child-raising duties to his wives and servants. Who could blame him, right?

And yet 1 Kings 1:6 strongly implies that David *could* have and *should* have participated in his son's rearing in a way that might have put the young man on a positive track leading to a longer, healthier, more significant life. Yes, Adonijah committed the sin that led to his death; but David had never, "at any time," corrected his son and said firmly to him, "No, you can't have everything that you see. You need to start putting others ahead of yourself, especially as a prince."

The disciples of Jesus, "the twelve," were no strangers to remaining silent when they needed to speak up. On one trip when they all passed through Galilee, Jesus told his men, "The Son of Man is being betrayed into the hands of men, and they will kill Him. And after He is killed, He will rise the third day" (Mark 9:31). This isn't trivial information, but it went right over the heads of the twelve. So how did they respond? Apparently they didn't want to risk embarrassment or a rebuke for dullness of mind, for Scripture says, "But they did not understand this saying, and were afraid to ask Him" (verse 32). In other words, they kept their mouths shut. They were silent when they should have spoken.

Shortly afterward, the group arrived in Capernaum and started settling into the house they were going to use as their base of operations. Jesus looked at them and asked, "What was it you disputed among yourselves on the road?" (verse 33). They thought He hadn't noticed! Scripture says, "They kept silent, for on the road they had disputed among themselves who would be the greatest" (verse 34).

Silence again—this time no doubt because of feelings of guilt, humiliation, shame, and the shock of being found out. Men generally don't like being unmasked! Jesus, however, was—and still is—an expert at unveiling the truth.

Our Lord wants you to engage. He wants you to speak up. He wants to move a lot of your conversations from the "unspoken" category to the "spoken" category. And He wants to do this not because He wishes to make you uncomfortable, but because it's one of the best ways He has to help you become the man, the husband, the father, and the mature spiritual leader He knows you really want to be.

ONLY HEAVEN KNOWS

Only heaven will reveal the problems, troubles, heartbreaks, and difficulties that have come our way as a result of our inability or unwillingness to speak what we'd rather leave unspoken.

First and foremost, stubborn silence and a persistent lack of communication damage our relationship with God. The Bible tells us that the Lord of the Universe ponders our way, seeks our hearts, and sees our paths. He wants to hear regularly from us, and He also desires that we regularly communicate with the other human beings He's made in His image and has put in our paths.

Second, I have found that when my relationship with God is not right, the breakdown affects my marriage, my relationships with my children, and even my relationships with my friends and coworkers.

Sin is not just a missing of the mark; it's an infection that spreads to every area of life. Although we don't always leave important things unspoken because of sin, since we live on a fallen planet and walk around in bodies that naturally want to do what the flesh desires, any failure to speak a necessary word—regardless of why we remain silent—plays into the enemy's hands. And so an innocent failure to speak up at the right time can lead very quickly to something far less innocent.

No doubt this is why God's Word instructs us, "Keep your heart with all diligence, for out of it spring the issues of life" (Proverbs 4:23). Another version says, "Above all else, guard your heart, for everything you do flows from it" (NIV). In other words, the condition of your heart will determine how your life turns out—and a very close connection exists between your heart and your mouth.

Jesus emphasized this connection when He said, "Out of the abundance of the heart the mouth speaks" (Matthew 12:34), and "those things which proceed out of the mouth come from the heart, and they defile a man" (Matthew 15:18). This ought to tell us that what we speak, as well as what we refuse or neglect to say, reveals a great deal about the condition of our heart. And once again, if we desire to grow as men dedicated to honoring and serving Christ, then we cannot afford to neglect our "word life."

I've walked alongside thousands of men in a pastoral ministry stretching over several decades, and I've seen what happens when men bury their true thoughts and feelings, refusing to speak what needs to be said. They remain trapped in bondage, sometimes for months, years, even whole lifetimes.

But why? It doesn't have to be that way. Biology doesn't have to keep us from the destiny God has marked out for us. Neither does culture. Neither does family history. We don't have to let *anything* get in the way of us becoming the men God had in mind when He created us, and that includes what may be the two biggest forces that tend to glue our mouths shut. Let's consider the first of those two forces next.

May the rams no longer be so silent!

2

BREAK THE
CHAINS OF FEAR

I t all began with a short phone call. She had not heard anything from this friend for more than a quarter of a century, and while the call would last only a few minutes, it would radically change her life and marriage—perhaps for as long as she lived.

While the friend's utter lack of opening pleasantries puzzled her, she understood the reason soon enough. The trembling voice on the other end of the line quickly began to unfold a sordid story about an illicit relationship that had taken place in secrecy more than twenty-five years before. The relationship involved her husband…and the long-silent friend's now twenty-five-year-old son.

The adulterous pair had managed to keep their secret under wraps for all those years. But when the friend could no longer cope with her sin and deception, she sought out a counselor, to whom she came clean. Eventually she felt compelled to reveal her secret to the faithful woman she had kept in the dark for so long.

Can any of us imagine the horror of such a long-dormant revelation? Betrayal on steroids!

While the scandalous details of this account differ from the stories that typify most of our lives, the element of silence does not. Too often, fear causes us to remain quiet when we should speak up. Fear prompts us to close our mouths when we should open them. We probably wag our tongues as much as anyone when we debate who has the best team in college football, or whistle over Jim's new boat, or sit around with some good buddies at a barbecue. But when it comes to talking about the big things in life with the people who matter most to us, we tend to clam up.

Why is that? Why do so many men so strongly resist talking about the very issues that keep them in hiding? Why do we seem so unwilling to tell others important truths about ourselves? Why do we insist on remaining silent or uncommunicative when we ought to speak up?

Over the many years of my ministry, I've seen a lot of heartbreaking scenarios similar to the one recounted above. And more often than not, the same reason accounts for the silence: fear.

WHAT IF THE TRUTH GOT OUT?

A high percentage of the men I know who keep silent about the crucial issues of their lives—issues that really demand discussion, or even confession—keep quiet because *they fear the consequences of speaking up.* They may not even admit to themselves why they seal their lips, but on some level, they know *exactly* why they keep quiet.

They fear that if they admit the truth, they will lose something precious to them. Their fear takes all sorts of shapes. Consider just a few of the fears that I've seen keep men silent:

- Loss of relationship (spouse, friends, family, business associates)
- Loss of possessions (house, car, inheritance)
- Loss of influence
- Loss of comfort
- Loss of reputation
- Loss of employment
- Loss of power
- Loss of control
- Loss of privilege
- Loss of status

The list goes on and on. We fear embarrassment if people should discover the real truth. We fear being ridiculed. We fear financial consequences, or even punishment. Whatever the fear, we allow that fear to dominate us. We give in to its angry demands that we close our mouths. And then everyone suffers, including those we love the most.

IT'S NOTHING NEW

This tendency toward silence is nothing new, of course. It came into existence a nanosecond after sin did. As soon as Adam took a bite of the fruit that God had instructed him not to eat, he went into silent hiding.

When the Lord showed up in Eden during the cool of the day for His usual stroll with the human rulers of His creation, Adam and Eve silenced themselves in their hiding places. When God finally called out to Adam, "Where are you?" listen to the man's answer:

"I heard you in the garden, *and I was afraid*" (Genesis 3:10 NIV).

What did Adam fear? Consequences, certainly; God had told him that death would follow a single swallow of the forbidden fruit. Adam feared *loss*: loss of privilege, loss of position, loss of relationship, loss of life.

Our sin has kept us quiet and in hiding ever since.

Jacob, the grandson of Abraham, once got into a very difficult situation with his corrupt father-in-law, Laban. Jacob's fears eventually prompted him to pack up his family and belongings in the middle of the night and run away without saying a word. When Laban caught up with Jacob the next day, here's how Jacob explained himself:

"*I was afraid*" (Genesis 31:31).

What did Jacob fear? Loss of relationships, loss of wealth, loss of health, loss of status.

You can count the first king of Israel, Saul, as yet another man who allowed his deep insecurities to prompt him to act foolishly, and then to keep quiet about it. When the prophet Samuel confronted the king about a very public sin, Saul first denied it, then admitted it (sort of) while at the same time trying to excuse his behavior. He had "transgressed the commandment of the LORD," he admitted, but it really wasn't his fault. He sinned because...

"I feared the people" (1 Samuel 15:24).

What did Saul fear? Loss of power, loss of privilege, loss of influence, loss of status.

God knows that all of us men struggle with all kinds of fears. He also knows that our fears can drive us to keep our mouths closed at the very moment we most need to open them.

What kinds of fears tend to turn *you* into a silent male?

What if your wife were to find out about your addiction to pornography?

What if your secret gambling habit were to become known?

What if the IRS were to discover the creative accounting on your last tax return?

What if your boss were to learn about your on-the-job drinking?

What if your church family were to get wind of your explosive temper?

I don't know what kinds of fears may drive you to silence, but I do know two things for certain about your fear, whatever that fear may be:

1. You believe that keeping quiet about it will protect you.

2. Your silence eventually will make your problem *far* worse.

THE CONSEQUENCES OF SECRECY

Over and over again, the Bible deals with the consequences of living a life of secrecy. Proverbs 28:13 declares, "He who covers his sins will not prosper, but whoever confesses and forsakes them will have mercy." In this verse, Solomon almost seems to meditate on the words of his father, David, who many years before had written, "When I kept silent [about my sin], my bones grew old through my groaning all the day long. For day and night, Your hand was heavy upon me; my vitality was turned into the drought of summer" (Psalm 32:34).

It only stands to reason that if we commit our sin in secrecy, then the enemy of our soul will scheme to keep us in secrecy. He wants us to remain in hiding, to keep quiet. He convinces us that it's for the best. Why rock the boat?

For a while, this demonic strategy may seem to work. We feel relieved as long as no one suspects a thing. The further the unseemly incident recedes into the past, the more it looks like we're in the clear. At some point, usually (but not always), our fears start to subside.

The problem is, such a strategy always comes with a spring-loaded trapdoor. Jesus tells us the strategy can never work over the long term, because God Himself will one day spring that trapdoor:

> There is nothing concealed that will not be disclosed, or hidden that will not be made known. What you have said in the dark will be heard in the daylight, and what you have whispered in the ear in the inner rooms will be proclaimed from the roofs (Luke 12:2-3 NIV).

A friend of mine tells me that during his boyhood years, his mother had a favorite verse that she quoted whenever she suspected he might be up to something: "Be sure your sin will find you out" (Numbers 32:23). God gives us chance after chance to come clean, to admit the truth, to speak up and remain silent no longer. If we refuse, if we allow our fears to keep our mouths shut, eventually the time will come when our sin does find us out. Sometimes, even in this world, that sin gets proclaimed from the roofs.

Howard Manoian became a local celebrity in a small Normandy village when he began describing his war exploits on D-Day during World War II.[1] The American told anyone who'd listen how Germans wounded him twice after he parachuted into Sainte-Mère-Eglise, once getting shot by a machine gun and once by a Messerschmitt. He told of jumping out of airplanes just after midnight, of preventing Germans from crossing a strategically important bridge, of playing an important role in the infamous Operation Market Garden (the subject of the film *A Bridge Too Far*). He spoke proudly of his famous unit, Company A of the 1st Battalion, 505th Parachute Regiment, 82nd Airborne Division.

He eventually retired to Chef-du-Pont, where locals honored him with a plaque near the entrance to the village museum, dedicated to honoring the 82nd Airborne. The French government later presented him with the nation's highest award for bravery, the Legion d'Honneur.

Manoian took up a regular spot at the local pub, reminiscing about his war exploits. He also sold war memorabilia at local events, bending his customers' ears with his exciting tales.

And then came the proclamation from the roofs: It was all a lie.

A search of military records revealed that although Manoian did serve in Normandy, he was never a paratrooper. He was never a member of the 82nd Airborne Division. Actually, he joined the 33rd Chemical Decontamination Company in Florida in July 1943, which existed to decontaminate men and machines after any chemical attack. The men of the 33rd never ended up having to serve in that capacity, however. While they did make it to Utah Beach (by supply ship), they finished out the war at a supply dump in northern France, giving showers to bone-tired soldiers. In 1945, Manoian returned home to Massachusetts, where he became a police officer.

Manoian really did get hurt during his overseas military stint, but not by German bullets. He once accidentally broke his middle finger while "on standby" in England, and later bruised his hand in another accident.

Manoian's embellishments came to light in 2009 and quickly got broadcast around the world through stories in *The Boston Herald* and *The Daily Mail*. France quickly rescinded his Legion d' Honneur award and removed his name from museums and official records. Manoian died two years later at a VA hospital in Washington, DC, apparently without ever admitting his deceit. By all accounts, he was a great guy and wonderful storyteller who got trapped in his own false world.

I wonder: Do you ever feel trapped in your own false world?

Have you worked hard to get others to believe a lie about you, or have you worked equally hard to keep some unflattering truth about you from coming out? The Holy Spirit of God says to you, "It's time to come clean."

A LIBERATING PROMISE

One of my favorite New Testament books is 1 John. The apostle wrote,

> This is the message which we have heard from Him and
> declare to you, that God is light and in Him is no darkness

at all. If we say that we have fellowship with Him, and walk in darkness, we lie and do not practice the truth. But if we walk in the light as He is in the light, we have fellowship with one another, and the blood of Jesus Christ His Son cleanses us from all sin. If we say that we have no sin, we deceive ourselves, and the truth is not in us (1:5-7).

What a liberating truth! What an encouraging promise! As we bring our "covered" secrecy into the light, our dear Lord exposes it for what it is. At last, we become capable of seeing and admitting the ugly—but bondage-breaking—truth. When we bring that secret into the light, fear loses its power to keep us in slavery.

Do you fear what men may do to you if you tell that which has remained unspoken? If so, let me encourage you to remember Proverbs 29:25, which says, "Fear of man will prove to be a snare, but whoever trusts in the LORD is kept safe" (NIV).

Do you feel afraid to deliver some message you believe the Lord wants you to speak? If so, then remember Jesus's words to a frightened apostle Paul: "Do not be afraid; keep on speaking, do not be silent. For I am with you" (Acts 18:9-10 NIV).

Have you kept silent for a long time about some sin in your life, not speaking of it maybe even for decades, because you fear the consequences of what might happen should you break your silence? Then remember the words of almighty God through Isaiah the prophet:

> Whom have you so dreaded and feared
> that you have not been true to me,
> and have neither remembered me
> nor taken this to heart?
> Is it not because I have long been silent
> that you do not fear me? (Isaiah 57:11 NIV).

God realizes very well that sometimes we act in false ways to Him and fail to remember Him in part because we know He doesn't typically judge us immediately for our sin. That's what He means when He asks, "Is it not because I have long been silent that you do not fear me?"

God wants us to fear Him, but not because we're afraid of Him. He could easily expose our sin the moment we commit it, but He wants us to walk in righteousness because we love to do so, not because we're afraid we'll get walloped if we don't. Our heavenly Father intends to make us like His Son, Jesus Christ, who delights to do His Father's will. That is why our Lord frequently gives us time to choose to come clean.

What's keeping you from coming clean?

CAN YOU LAUGH AT YOURSELF?

I have often heard it said that the closer a person gets to Jesus, the less he thinks of himself. Such a spiritually growing man finds it increasingly easier to laugh at himself and harder to take himself too seriously because he knows the truth. And that truth doesn't scare him anymore.

An old story tells how the great medieval theologian St. Thomas Aquinas, who wrote a massive book of theology called the *Summa Theologica,* died and went to heaven. Shortly after he arrived, he was told that the famous book he wrote was nothing more than "straw." Do you know how Aquinas reacted, according to the story? He *laughed.* He found the assessment funny because he knew the truth about himself.

If it's true that the closer a person gets to Jesus the less he thinks of himself, then maybe the reverse is also true. Perhaps the further we get from God, the worse we feel about ourselves and the more we believe we will be disrespected if anyone were to know our secrets. That idea frightens us, and therefore, to retain some sense of our "manly dignity," we carefully manufacture a false image of ourselves. We keep quiet because we *want* others to believe a lie about us. We *want* them to think we're different than what we really are.

I know of a young man in his mid-twenties who once told a friend, "I don't want anyone to really know me." Everyone considered him a great and talented guy, somebody you'd want at parties and on your softball or basketball team. He attended church regularly, participated in a series of Bible study groups, and volunteered his time to help various causes. But true to his word, he never let anyone get too close. He would associate with one small group of "close friends" for a couple of years, and then he would move on to another group, and then another group, and then another. He started dating less and less and drinking more and more.

His life never "blew up," so far as I know, and he never became an alcoholic, so far as I know. But as he grew older, the borders of his life kept shrinking. He struggled with anger issues, felt confused by them, and grew increasingly isolated and alone. Eventually he considered pulling up the stakes from where he had lived for decades to move back to his hometown, hoping, perhaps, to find some of the camaraderie and happiness he remembered as a boy. What he really wanted and missed was close connection with others. But, of course, that *never* comes without a willingness to let others really know you. This man never moved away from his foolish (and fear-filled) statement, "I don't want anyone to really know me." And so the older he grew, the less satisfied he became with his life. So sad.

Does that sound anything like you? If you have a stronger commitment to your image than you do to the truth, then it may well sound *a lot* like you. If you're continuing to refuse to speak up about that dirty little secret in your life, then you can forget about ever experiencing true intimacy. Darkness tends to expand around secret sins, and intimacy needs light to grow.

A BETTER PATTERN TO FOLLOW

While the natural pattern may be to avoid the truth and instead create a false image, God gives us another option—a far better one. As I look at the New Testament, I see this better option clearly and powerfully modeled in the life of the apostle Paul.

When we describe Paul today, often we use words like *great* and *fearless* and *giant* and *successful*. By contrast, he usually chose a completely different set of words to describe himself. I have always called Paul the greatest missionary statesman who ever lived, apart from Jesus Himself. Yet take a look at Paul's own view of himself, as he frequently expressed it in Scripture:

- "Christ Jesus came into the world to save sinners, of whom I am chief" (1 Timothy 1:15).

- "To me, who am less than the least of all of the saints, this grace was given" (Ephesians 3:8).

- "I am the least of the apostles, who am not worthy to be called an apostle, because I persecuted the church of God" (1 Corinthians 15:9).

- "I am nothing" (2 Corinthians 12:11).

I find these self-descriptions remarkable, almost breathtaking. Paul didn't have a poor self-image, as some today might suggest. In the very same sentence he wrote, "I am nothing," he could also write, "I ought to have been commended by you, for I am not in the least inferior to the 'super-apostles,' even though I am nothing" (2 Corinthians 12:11 NIV).

Paul knew who he was, and he had no trouble admitting it. He was the apostle who had tried to destroy the church. He was a ground-breaking, globe-trotting missionary who knew himself as the worst of sinners. I find this spirit to be true not only of Paul, but also of godly men we admire throughout history. Consider William Carey, noted as the father of modern missions. On his seventieth birthday, after helping to translate the Bible into more than forty languages, this man of God who gave us the famous quote "Expect great things from God; attempt great things for God" used a single word to describe his Christian journey:

"Struggle."

In a letter to one of his sons, William wrote,

> I am this day 70 years old, a moment of Divine mercy and goodness, though on a review of my new life I find much, very much, for which I ought to be humbled in the dust. My direct and positive sins are immeasurable, my negligence in the Lord's work has been great, I have not promoted his cause, not sought his glory and honor as I ought. Notwithstanding all of this, I am spared till now, and am

still retained in his work, and I trust I am received into the divine favor through him.[2]

Men like the apostle Paul and William Carey have learned that the way up is the way down. Christ lifts them up when they admit how they have fallen down.

Have you learned this secret? Do you make it a regular practice to confess your sins so that the Spirit of God may break the power of darkness in your life? Or are you allowing your fear of being "found out" to keep you silent, keep you afraid, keep you in bondage? The Bible instructs us, urges us, and encourages us to confess our wrongdoing, whatever it may be. James, the half-brother of our Lord, wrote, "Confess your trespasses to one another, and pray for one another, that you may be healed. The effective, fervent prayer of a righteous man avails much" (James 5:16).

Don't let fear turn you into a coward. Choose health and freedom!

TIME TO COME CLEAN

Over the years I have felt deeply encouraged by so many, especially in ministry, who have called to share with me some victory won in their life as a result of being transparently honest.

I recently received a call from a young pastor in Kentucky who told me about the many struggles he had endured as a result of making several bad choices. After he committed these sins, he struggled for a long time with coming clean about them. He felt tremendous fear about the consequences that he imagined would follow any such confession, and so for many months he resisted becoming honest and open about what he had done.

But this is where the story gets so encouraging.

Once this young man made the courageous decision to uncover his sins by confessing them to his wife, he essentially held his breath. What would happen? Would he get blasted with the consequences he most feared?

Certainly his wife felt hurt by his ugly revelation. She also expressed overwhelming curiosity about why on *earth* he would make such foolish choices. But upon observing his genuine brokenness over this sin and his willingness to be transparent, she quickly laid his worst fears to rest. She even told him that she believed his confession would help them to build a wonderful path for a life full of genuine intimacy.

"Telling my wife was the best thing I ever did," he told me. "I felt shocked by the grace she showed to me—but even more by the way she loved me."

The enemy would have you believe that living a lie is better than the truth, but Jesus insists that only truth has the power to set you free. This young preacher is now prospering, even though the Bible teaches us that the person who covers his sin will *not* prosper. So how is that possible?

This is nothing else but the good news of the gospel. Any sin we *un*cover, the Lord then covers. As His Word promises, "Love covers a multitude of sins" (1 Peter 4:8 ESV).

At the same time, I have to say that when we delay dealing with our sin, that delay can leave scars—even when that sin is forgiven. The very nature of sin is to kill, and if you don't kill it first, it can leave you with a graveyard filled with a mountain of regrets. As I wrote this chapter, I received the following words in a text from a friend:

> My thoughts bring back a lot of painful memories, of boundaries not set, foolish choices, painful consequences. I know God has forgiven me, and you, along with my family, have been forgiving and so kind. I know I do not want any man to experience the pain, heartache, broken relationship, deep sorrow, and regret like I have experienced, and still deal with at times. I am with family, but still lonely inside. I miss having a wife, companion, lover, and friend to enjoy life's journey. I am trying to look forward to being a good Dad, Grandpa, and friend and being open to help wherever I can.
>
> I have told others to fly long distance to visit me since my divorce if they want to seek counsel for their own troubled marriages.

Grateful and humble that God would use someone who is so broken and still hurting at times.

Could it be that our Lord might want to use a brief look into someone else's story to arrest our hearts and cause us to come clean…before our own story appears in someone else's book?

Pride:
The Ultimate Path
to Self-Destruction

A friend of mine insists he's insane.

He's not locked up (yet), and no psychiatric review board is debating whether to put him in state custody. Most of the time, he goes about his life as any other sane man would. He works hard, pays his bills, takes his family to church, burns stuff on the grill, exercises at the gym, and gets along decently with his neighbors.

That is, until he goes insane.

This tends to occur, he says, whenever his iPad goes missing, or he can't find the remotes to the TV or DVD player, or his car keys have vanished, or some item he needs for work has disappeared from the spot he *knew* he put it the day before. His madness typically begins with irritation, which quickly builds to a minor temper tantrum. He storms around the house, huffing and spluttering and talking to himself as his anger mounts.

"I *told* them to put that back where it belongs!" he mutters. "If they can't take care of this thing—*MY* thing—then they can't use it at all!! I'm going to lock it up or hide it where only *I* can get to it!"

You may think, *Johnny, that's not insanity. That's just fatherly wrath. Family life does that to us.* While I won't disagree with you, I have to tell you that I haven't started to describe the insanity part yet. That comes a little later.

Eventually my friend goes on to confront one or more of the guilty parties.

"How many *times* do I have to *tell* you to *put my stuff back where it belongs?*" he thunders. "I get so *tired* of hunting for these things *all* over the house! If you can't take care of my stuff, then you can't use it anymore! Do I make myself *clear?!*"

Most of the time, his chastened children and his concerned wife set about to earnestly look for the missing items; but sadly, nobody can remember where the lost items might have ended up. He stomps around some more while they silently search under pillows, beneath piles of letters, and behind coats or doors.

And then, usually within a few minutes, the insanity hits.

My friend looks in a neglected spot and there finds his thoughtlessly discarded items…exactly where *he* put them. The jarring truth immediately comes rushing back. But does he tell his wife? Does he ask her forgiveness for unjustly accusing her? Does he admit to his children that he, and not them, was the culprit? Well, not *always*.

Does that make any sense? Is that sane behavior—to know the truth but to withhold the information? Especially when you recognize that this exact scenario plays out perhaps 95 to 98 percent of the time? And that this very same insanity unfolds not once in a great while, not just every now and then, but several times a year, maybe as often as once a month?

Is that *sane*?

If you were this man, wouldn't it be the rational thing to suppose that *you* had somehow misplaced your keys, or left your iPad in an odd spot, or dropped the remotes wherever you happened to place them once you finished watching your game? Why would you assume—every time, without fail—that someone else had made off with the items, either with evil or at least inconsiderate intent?

But the insanity gets worse—a lot worse. This friend admits that too often he would rather have his beloved family believe a lie than tell them the truth. He'd rather they go to bed feeling guilty for misplacing his stuff than admit he was the blameworthy party. Now, I know my friend loves his family. I know he loves God. I know he loves both the gospel and the truth. So how is this crazy behavior not insane?

It makes me wonder: What drives such a man to avoid telling the truth? What keeps him silent when he should speak up? What stops him from immediately admitting to his wife or kids, "Ah, heh heh, *funny* thing, it turns out I found my keys [iPad, remotes, work stuff] exactly where I left them"? I think the answer comes down to one word: Pride.

A COMPETITION MEN CAN'T STAND TO LOSE

I'm convinced that pride is one of the most potent forces keeping Christian men's mouths shut when these brothers should speak up. Their pride gets in the way of the truth, and so they remain silent.

Why? They feel embarrassed. They feel foolish. They feel like losers, as though they've just lost a very public competition. They don't want anyone to laugh at them, to look at them and snicker. They're winners, after all, and they want to make sure everyone treats them like one.

Regardless of the truth.

C.S. Lewis hinted at this a long time ago in his classic book *Mere Christianity*. He called pride "the complete anti-God state of mind"[1] and saw it as fundamentally competitive. He pointed out that "each person's pride is in competition with everyone else's pride. It is because I wanted to be the big noise at the party that I am so annoyed at someone else being the big noise."[2] And he observed,

> Pride is essentially competitive—is competitive by its very nature—while the other vices are competitive only, so to speak, by accident. Pride gets no pleasure out of having something, only out of having more of it than the next man. We say that people are proud of being rich, or clever, or good-looking, but they are not. They are proud of being richer, or cleverer, or better-looking than others. If someone else became equally rich, or clever, or good-looking there would be nothing to be proud about. It is the comparison that makes you proud: the pleasure of being above the rest. Once the element of competition has gone, pride has gone.[3]

Very likely this unpleasant reality explains the root of my friend's insanity. In those crazy moments, he sees himself as competing with his wife and kids. If they win, he loses—so even if it turns out he didn't win, he doesn't want *them* to know it. He might even admit his little secret to a buddy at work or to a neighborhood friend, but why not? They're not competitors, at least at home. But to admit to his wife, "Honey, I'm sorry, but I'm the one who misplaced my keys, not you"? He feels repulsed at making such a clear declaration of defeat. And so he remains silent.

A COMMON BIBLICAL PICTURE

We see the same pattern throughout Scripture. What, for example, do you suppose went through Adam's mind after he and Eve ate the forbidden fruit, and then God showed up in the garden? God knew what they had done, of course, and certainly He knew where they were. But the guilt-ridden humans hid from the Lord and kept quiet.

So God asked Adam, "Where are you?" (Genesis 3:9). Adam finally broke his silence, but in the end, he did so only to throw his wife under the bus (if there had been buses in those days). If someone had to lose, Adam reasoned, he wanted it to be her, not him. And so he blurted out to the Lord, "The woman whom You gave to be with me, she gave me of the tree, and I ate" (Genesis 3:12). Not my fault, Sir. Blame her.

What is that, if not pride, pure and simple? Unvarnished, unbridled, unlovely pride. Pride kept Adam silent at first, and then pride urged him to make his wife a worse loser than he was. This didn't mean he had "won" by any means, but at least he thought he had avoided coming in last place.

And what about King David? God Himself had called this former shepherd "a man after My own heart" (Acts 13:22). And yet David fell into the sins of both adultery and murder. Then he kept silent about his sordid choices for a whole year. The king himself later admitted to God, "When I kept silent, my bones wasted away through my groaning all day long. For day and night your hand was heavy upon me; my strength was sapped as in the heat of summer" (Psalm 32:3-4 NIV).

Tellingly, though, *none* of that prompted David to open his mouth and admit his wickedness—not decaying bones, not twenty-four-hour whimpering, not a withering hand of divine judgment, not physical weakness as bad as that of a sunstroke victim. (A little later, we'll get to what *did* prompt him.)

What kept David so silent for so long? He might have feared the consequences for his despicable actions, but his words lead me to think another cause kept his mouth shut and his heart hardened. An ancient note describes Psalm 51 as "A psalm of David. When the prophet Nathan came to him after David had committed adultery with Bathsheba." While we shouldn't consider these historical notes as inspired as the biblical text itself, we have good reason to believe the accuracy of this description. The whole psalm calls on God's goodness and mercy and compassion to wash away David's guilt once he confessed his sin. It talks about the joy that God restores to a repentant sinner, and David asks the Lord to "open my lips, and my mouth shall show forth Your praise" (verse 15).

So what had kept those royal lips sealed for so long? David gives us a big clue when he writes, "The sacrifices of God are a broken spirit, a broken and contrite heart—these, O God, You will not despise" (verse 17). Two times in this short verse, David uses the word *broken*. Not until he had a "broken" spirit and a "broken" and contrite heart did the king find forgiveness for his sin and a sure path back to joy. So the question is this: What about David's spirit and his heart needed to be "broken"?

You can break only that which is hard, unyielding. And *nothing* makes the human heart and spirit harder than pride. That's why centuries later, when Nehemiah was in prayer, he would use the following words to describe his sinful, unrepentant ancestors: "They became arrogant and disobeyed your commands. They sinned against your ordinances…Stubbornly they turned their backs on you, became stiff-necked and refused to listen" (Nehemiah 9:29 NIV). A stiff neck needs to be broken. A hard heart must be shattered. Otherwise, they clog up the ears and make it impossible for repentance and confession to take root.

THREE SYMPTOMS OF PRIDE

The Bible makes it clear that a man's pride does several nasty things to him. Let's take a brief look at just a few of the worst symptoms. By no means does the following present an exhaustive list! But I hope it helps to convince you of how serious a problem pride really is for any man.

Although many Scripture verses describe how human pride leads to boasting, cursing, and lies, I want to focus here on how pride also leads to an ungodly silence that ends up destroying both men and their loved ones. In my own experience, I'd probably say that for every boorish, loudmouthed boaster I've encountered, I've observed maybe a dozen smug, closed-mouthed egotists. Both groups are in deep trouble. Consider what God has to say about how pride warps a man's character and eventually destroys him. Pride prompts a man to…

1. Refuse to Listen to Wisdom or Correction

Note how God's Word contrasts human pride with God's wisdom, and how pride causes a man to close his ears to what God says: "Where there is strife, there is pride, but wisdom is found in those who take advice" (Proverbs 13:10 NIV). The men of ancient Israel continually struggled to bridle their pride, and their failure to listen to divine correction cost them dearly:

> Hear and give ear; be not proud, for the LORD has spoken.
> Give glory to the LORD your God before he brings darkness,
> before your feet stumble on the twilight mountains, and
> while you look for light he turns it into gloom and makes it
> deep darkness. But if you will not listen, my soul will weep
> in secret for your pride; my eyes will weep bitterly and run
> down with tears, because the LORD's flock has been taken
> captive (Jeremiah 13:15-17 ESV).

> For many years you were patient with them. By your Spirit
> you admonished them through your prophets. Yet they
> paid no attention, so you handed them over to the neigh-
> boring peoples (Nehemiah 9:30 NIV).

> They refused to pay attention; stubbornly they turned their

backs and covered their ears. They made their hearts as hard as flint and would not listen to the law or to the words that the LORD Almighty had sent by his Spirit through the earlier prophets. So the LORD Almighty was very angry (Zechariah 7:11-12 NIV).

2. *Refuse to Submit to God's Word*

Pride not only stops up a man's ears, it also shuts down his heart. A proud man is like King Jehoiakim, who had scribes read to him a scroll Jeremiah the prophet had written. After every three or four columns were read, the king used a knife to cut off the words and casually toss them into a fire (Jeremiah 36:23). We were made for fellowship with God, but pride makes that fellowship impossible:

> Turn at my rebuke; surely I will pour out my spirit on you; I will make my words known to you. Because I have called and you refused, I have stretched out my hand and no one regarded, because you disdained all my counsel, and would have none of my rebuke, I also will laugh at your calamity; I will mock when your terror comes, when your terror comes like a storm, and your destruction comes like a whirlwind, when distress and anguish come upon you (Proverbs 1:23-27).

> The LORD, the God of their ancestors, sent word to them through his messengers again and again, because he had pity on his people and on his dwelling place. But they mocked God's messengers, despised his words and scoffed at his prophets until the wrath of the LORD was aroused against his people and there was no remedy (2 Chronicles 36:15-16 NIV).

3. *Refuse to Admit Wrongdoing*

Pride not only stops up a man's ears and shuts down his heart, it also closes his mouth. A proud man refuses to admit his wrong. "You have heard these things; look at them all," the Lord said to his stubborn people in Judah. "Will you not admit them?" (Isaiah 48:6 NIV). A contemporary of Isaiah, Hosea, had a similar word for God's people in the northern kingdom: "For I will be like a lion to Ephraim, and like a young lion to the house of Judah. I, even I, will tear them away, and no one shall rescue. I will return again to My place till they acknowledge their offense" (Hosea 5:14-15).

PRIDE MEANS OPPOSITION TO GOD

Pride is catastrophic for every man because it absolutely opposes grace—and therefore opposes God Himself. The Bible is filled with texts like this one: "The fear of the LORD is to hate evil; pride and arrogance and the evil way and the perverse mouth I hate" (Proverbs 8:13). The proud and arrogant cannot, by definition, fear the Lord. It's impossible. Proud men can be very religious, but they cannot be godly.

"The LORD detests all the proud of heart," says Proverbs 16:5. "Be sure of this: They will not go unpunished" (NIV). And if that doesn't sound strong enough for you, listen to just a couple more like it:

> Whom have you reproached and blasphemed? Against whom have you raised your voice, and lifted up your eyes on high? Against the Holy One of Israel! (Isaiah 37:23).

> God resists the proud, but gives grace to the humble (James 4:6).

Why does God oppose the proud? Those who are prideful hate the truth and turn from it; they keep silent and walk away. By contrast, the humble love the truth, regardless of whatever ugly (but accurate) things it may tell them about themselves. So Peter wrote, "All of you, clothe yourselves with humility toward one another, because, 'God opposes the proud but shows favor to the humble'" (1 Peter 5:5 NIV).

The worst thing about pride is that it puts you at loggerheads with God. C.S. Lewis explained,

> In God you come up against something which is in every respect immeasurably superior to yourself. Unless you know God as that—and, therefore, know yourself as nothing in comparison—you do not know God at all. As long as you are proud you cannot know God. A proud man is

always looking down on things and people: and, of course, as long as you are looking down, you cannot see something that is above you.[4]

God hates a man's pride because it separates that man from Himself. A proud man—whether boastful or silent—focuses so much on himself that he cannot focus anywhere else. Listen to Lewis one final time:

> We must not think Pride is something God forbids because He is offended at it, or that Humility is something He demands as due to His own dignity—as if God Himself was proud. He is not in the least worried about His dignity. The point is, He wants you to know Him: wants to give you Himself. And He and you are two things of such a kind that if you really get into any kind of touch with Him you will, in fact, be humble—delightedly humble, feeling the infinite relief of having for once got rid of all the silly nonsense about your own dignity which has made you restless and unhappy all your life. He is trying to make you humble in order to make this moment possible: trying to take off a lot of silly, ugly, fancy-dress in which we have all got ourselves up and are strutting about like the little idiots we are…To get even near it [humility], even for a moment, is like a drink of cold water to a man in a desert.[5]

But how do you get a drink of cold water to a man in a desert? It's not easy. Oftentimes you can't confront a proud man directly because direct confrontation may only stoke the man's pride, making it more difficult for him to get to the place he needs to be. In other words, giving him more information is not usually the solution. So how do you pierce the pride and soften the man's heart?

RELEASING A GODLY MAN TRAPPED BY PRIDE

We could do a lot worse than to mimic God's own strategies when He works in a man's life to break down his pride and get him back into a healthy place of humble fellowship. So what does God do? One of his key strategies involves *indirect* communication—not confronting the problem directly, but through a side door, so to speak.

Much of the time, a proud man doesn't suffer from a lack of information, but from intense personal resistance to the information he already has. In those cases, the Lord often graciously crafts an indirect approach that may take more time than a direct assault, but which bears a lot more fruit. This is what He did with David after the king committed adultery with Bathsheba and arranged for the death of her husband, Uriah.

A direct approach might suggest, "Let the king have it with both barrels! Tell him he sinned and demand that he repent publicly. Threaten him with divine retribution. Scorch him but good!" That is not, however, what God did.

In fact, the Lord led the prophet Nathan to a much more indirect approach (you can read about it in 2 Samuel 12). Nathan told the king a story about a wealthy tycoon who had defrauded a poor man of something precious to him just because the rich dude didn't want to dip into his own vast resources. The story both engaged and enraged David—and then Nathan calmly told the king, "You are the man!" Nathan used a story about another man to prompt the guilty, proud king to reconnect with his better self and so finally be able to confess his own despicable actions. The crafting and telling of a story—an indirect method—led directly to David's repentance and restoration.

What might have happened had Nathan tried a more direct approach? Perhaps the prophet remembered Goliath's severed head and opted for a different strategy.

An indirect strategy, of course, tends to take a lot more thought and planning than does most direct communication. Could that be why we don't take that path very often? If you know a Christian man consumed by pride, however—a man who knows better but has allowed pride to take control of him—then maybe it's time for you to consider using an indirect approach to help him reconnect with the truth and with God.

Let me sketch out for you five indirect approaches that we see used repeatedly in Scripture:

1. Telling stories to get past defenses and connect emotionally with the hearer.

While the account of David and Nathan might be the classic one in this category, the same approach appears throughout both testaments. I think immediately of Jesus's frequent use of parables (short stories). He explained to His disciples that He spoke to the crowds

> in parables, because seeing they do not see, and hearing they do not hear, nor do they understand. Indeed, in their case the prophecy of Isaiah is fulfilled that says: "You will indeed hear but never understand, and you will indeed see but never perceive." For this people's heart has grown dull, and with their ears they can barely hear, and their eyes they have closed, lest they should see with their eyes and hear with their ears and understand with their heart and turn, and I would heal them" (Matthew 13:13-15 ESV).

Pride dulls a man's heart and closes his ears. Sometimes a well-crafted story can pierce that pride and lead to healing.

2. Asking questions to engage a man's curiosity.

Have you ever considered how often in Scripture God and His servants ask questions? From the first book of the Bible to the last, questions arise—not so much to gain information, but to get their audience to consider in a new way their (often grim) situation and their (frequently poor) choices. Questions have the power to pierce a man's defensive armor in a way that declarative statements cannot.

3. Stated concealment.

I have wondered if one of Jesus's most important but least-echoed strategies is found in this revealing admission: "I still have many things to say to you, but you cannot bear them now" (John 16:12). Jesus saw no point in inundating His audience with information. He gave His men what He knew they could handle...and then He stopped. At the same time, He told them they would find out more in the future, at some unknown time, once they had the ability to process it. This strategy places a mystery within a man's mind that sometimes bears fruit later. *What did He mean when He said He can't tell me now? Why can't I bear it? What does He have to say that He wants to tell me later?*

4. *Use of figurative language and actions.*

Perhaps the Old Testament champion in this category is Ezekiel, who acted in many symbolic and even odd ways to try to get the attention of his proud, unrepentant countrymen. He dug through Jerusalem's wall to symbolize a coming disaster. He laid siege to a model city for more than a year to symbolize a coming invasion. He packed up his things and moved to another location to picture the coming exile. He used wild, unconventional language to arrest the attention of his fellow Hebrews and so, he hoped, prompt them to change their ways. One verse captures the essence of this strategy: "Perhaps they will understand, though they are a rebellious house" (Ezekiel 12:3 NIV). In the New Testament, I think immediately of the arresting words spoken by Jesus—"drink my blood…eat my flesh" (see John 6:51-55)—and of the odd episode with Peter involving sheets, unclean animals, and a strange command (see Acts 10). Sometimes it takes mysterious, unconventional language and actions to help a man "understand" his situation. If you don't first capture his attention (and his imagination), then how are you going to help him to seriously reconsider his current life trajectory?

5. *Let him overhear a conversation.*

Sometimes a man needs to hear words really meant for another. Suppose a very busy dad arrives home early one day and overhears his little girls playing in another room. "I'll be the mommy," says one daughter to the other, "and you be the daddy." After a pause, the dad hears his younger daughter reply, "No, I don't want to be the daddy. Daddies are never home. I want to be Uncle Jim instead."

Do you think overhearing that conversation would have more of an effect on the man than his wife telling him directly, "You need to spend more time with your girls"? God understands this strategy and uses it, so why don't we?

I think of fearful Gideon before he led the Israelites against a much larger enemy. God told him he'd succeed, but Gideon still wavered. So

God arranged for him to overhear a conversation between two foreigners. "If you are afraid to attack," God said to Gideon, "go down to the camp with your servant Purah and listen to what they are saying. Afterward, you will be encouraged to attack the camp" (Judges 7:10-11). So that's what he did. And here's what he overheard: "I had a dream," one enemy soldier told another. "A round loaf of barley bread came tumbling into the Midianite camp. It struck the tent with such force that the tent overturned and collapsed." The man's companion replied, "This can be nothing other than the sword of Gideon son of Joash, the Israelite. God has given the Midianites and the whole camp into his hands" (verses 13-14).

Sometimes, a proud man in your life needs to overhear a conversation meant for someone else. That can be the key that unlocks a stubborn door.

We need to keep at least three things in mind whenever we utilize an indirect communication strategy. First, realize that it takes time. Results don't always come immediately, or even overnight. Sometimes it takes a while for the message to seep in and have a positive effect. And sometimes the man isn't quite ready for it yet; it may take months for the proper moment to arrive.

Second, this strategy offers no guarantee that it will work. In Ezekiel's day, God Himself is the one who said, "*Perhaps* they will understand." Some men will, some won't. But more may well understand through such an indirect method than through a direct confrontation.

Third, you can't approach a proud man with a club. You have to come to him humbly, giving up your claims, heedless of your possibly weak appearance or lack of public esteem. *You* can't be the message. You're just the messenger boy.

ON A SANER TRACK

Remember my friend with the intermittent case of insanity? I'm glad to say he's recovering. He's not cured yet, but he's on his way. Do you know one of the things that put him on a saner track? A story.

He heard one day about a ministry leader who did a 360-degree evaluation of his leadership. When he received back the anonymous appraisals of his management style, he read repeatedly of an authoritarian man who blustered and bullied his subordinates to get his way. He read of a would-be-king who always thought any problems in the organization could be traced to others, never to himself. And at the very next meeting of this organization's leadership team, he stood up, threw the 360-degree evaluation document on the table, and declared, "This is not me. End of story." And he went right on being the authoritarian bully he'd always been.

My friend did not want to become that bully. And so he admitted his pride and arrogance to his wife and kids, repented, and determined to take a different path. Oh, he still loses his keys, his remotes, his iPad, and his office stuff. And he is still quick to assume that someone in his household has misplaced them. But then he checks himself, remembers his history, and calms down. Once in a while, someone other than my friend really *has* mislaid the missing item. But he has lessened the number of times he runs around and accuses others of theft and threatens to hide his treasures. Peace reigns under his roof a lot more these days.

And peace makes a *much* more pleasant home than pride.

PART 2:

WHERE SILENCE
IS KILLING US

4

Brain Ruts

In October 2015, *Cosmopolitan* magazine published an article titled "Eight Reasons Watching Porn Doesn't Make Him a Cheater." It tried to make readers feel good about watching pornography, almost ridiculing anyone who would stand against it.

More than a decade earlier, the phenomenally popular TV sitcom *Friends* (still in wide syndication) made a running joke out of the habitual use of pornography by the show's leading male characters. The sitcom, rated number 21 on *TV Guide's* "50 Greatest Shows of All Time," casually presented pornography as something fun, harmless, and completely normal. No one blushed about Joey or Chandler's infatuation with porn. It was just something else to talk and joke about.

Although statistics tell us that a huge percentage of Christian guys have bought into the lies of the *Cosmo* article and the *Friends* schtick— they consume pornography at basically the same rates and levels as non-Christians—these believers *do* blush. They feel ashamed of their viewing habits and therefore don't speak about them. They keep quiet about their dirty little secret, and so it remains hidden underground.

But that can't stop it from ruining their lives.

THE FACTS ON PORN

Did you know that porn sites receive more regular traffic than Netflix, Amazon, and Twitter combined? About 35 percent of all Internet downloads, more than one out of every three, are porn-related.

About 34 percent of Internet users have been exposed to unwanted porn through ads and pop-ups. Some 2.5 billion emails each day have porn in them.[1]

The most common female role in porn is women in their twenties portraying teenagers. Child porn is one of the fastest-growing online businesses in the world; it is a $3 billion a year industry.[2]

Males are first exposed to pornography, on average, in the preteen years. The statistics vary from study to study, but the age range runs from 8 years to 13 years. Maybe an older sibling puts porn on his smartphone and his younger brother unknowingly opens the browser, only to find *that*. My cousin introduced me to pornography when I was twelve.

As the pastor of a large church, I have tens of thousands of followers on Twitter, Facebook, and Instagram. I don't know exactly how many followers I have and I don't check up on what they do. But my security people do. One day, security called me and said, "You need to go on your site and block some followers."

"Why?" I asked.

"Some pornographic people are following you," they said.

Well, glory to God, I thought, *I'm glad they're following me, because they're going to be reading all of my gospel devotions.* But after I did my research, I had to ask a question: *Why* were they following me? In fact, they hoped I'd find and follow *them*. I blocked their access.

I don't recall the exact words, but I remember Adrian Rogers saying something to this effect: "If you turn on the television and it's on a bad station and there's a lady undressed, the average man, even if he's filled with the Holy Ghost of God, it's gonna take all of the Holy Ghost of God in him to change the channel." And television isn't the only problem. Smartphones today have access to many millions of pornographic images. Just click the button!

Let's get honest: We're made that way. God created us with our sexuality. God created it for good, for pleasure, for procreation. But we *have* to get a handle on it.

Statistically, there's no difference between believers and nonbelievers in how frequently both groups view porn. Back in 2015, an article carried the title "Pornography Use Among Self-Identified Christians Largely Mirrors National Average, Survey Finds."[3] The survey revealed that 67 percent of men between the ages of thirty-one and forty-nine view porn monthly, and 49 percent of men from fifty to sixty-eight years of age view it monthly.

Even pastors struggle. According to the Barna Group, 57 percent of pastors admit to using porn, and 64 percent of youth pastors.[4] Do you know one of the major reasons missions agencies are unable to send potential recruits overseas? It's addiction to porn.

The question is no longer, Have you viewed porn? But rather, Have you managed your challenge with porn?

THE EFFECTS OF PORN

The sobering truth is that what you put into your mind, you will act out and ultimately become. Second Corinthians 3:18 tells us that when you love Jesus and the family of God and you desire to grow to spiritual maturity, you become more like Jesus. In a similar (but opposite) way, when you spend hours on the Internet addicted to porn, you become more like the smut you watch.

Pornography erodes your confidence and self-worth—it makes you feel lonely. You may stand out in a crowd, you may even be outgoing. But deep in your heart, you feel desperately lonely.

An addiction to pornography makes you feel shame and self-condemnation. It causes you to hide. The enemy will lie to you, and you'll find yourself affirming every one of those lies.

Pornography also stunts your emotional and spiritual growth. It keeps you immature by creating a radical self-centeredness. We live in an era that encourages us to do whatever comes into our minds, whatever we want to do. It's all about *me*. We live in the most self-centered culture ever to blight the planet. It's all about what we want, what we imagine we need. We ask, "What's okay for *me*?"

An addiction to pornography therefore brings about emotional and relational immaturity—you stop growing in relationships. Its unhealthy view of sex will give you a self-centered and self-gratifying view of *all* relationships, marriage included. You'll find yourself unable to satisfy the mate God brought into your life. Even worse, perhaps, you'll want your spouse to act out and measure up to what you've absorbed on the Internet. You'll also feel a continual, strong temptation to go even further, eventually leading to sexual aggression. It's just a matter of time.

All of this leads to a long, steady march in the wrong direction. It's nothing but old-fashioned deception that grows in secret. An addiction to pornography thrives in the dark, and that darkness has its sights set on those who have been called to live in the light.

TARGET: CHRISTIAN COMMUNITIES

The porn industry knows that it cannot survive unless more users become addicted to its material. The search for new users is widespread, and it even targets Christians—not only to gain new customers, but to silence criticism of its industry. They know that Christians who view porn aren't as likely to speak out against it—while the shame that comes from viewing porn is great, the shame of hypocrisy is too.

Pornographers want more than your money; they want your allegiance, both body and soul. And if you call yourself an evangelical Christian, they've drawn a big target on your back.

THE SCIENCE OF BRAIN RUTS

In an article titled "Why 68% of Men in Church Watch Porn," according to Dr. Ted Roberts, churches often treat the issue of consuming pornography as strictly a moral failure, thus failing to recognize it primarily as a brain problem. In fact, the strongest sex organ in the human body is the brain.

"We tell men to try harder, pray harder, and love Jesus more…But, what starts off as a moral problem, quickly becomes a brain problem. Telling a man to try harder is only tightening the 'noose' of bondage."[5]

Researchers who have studied cognitive brain function have helped to reveal how mental strongholds develop and how a person becomes enslaved to something like pornography. According to psychologist Dr.

Tim Jennings, author of *The God-Shaped Brain,* when a mother breast-feeds her child, her brain releases powerful hormones that bond her to that child. When a man watches porn, the same powerful chemicals get released, which bonds him to those images.[6] This is why Satan so viciously attacks our sexuality. In doing that, the devil actively inter-feres with human bonding. *Any* type of repetitive behavior creates trails or ruts in the brain that will fire on an automatic sequence. The result is years of bondage.

This helps to explain how 68 percent of Christian men can love the Lord with all their heart, but still get trapped in sexual bondage. A Christian man does not get addicted to pornography simply because he stops loving God. I refuse to believe such nonsense.

Repeated viewing of porn actually changes the physical structure of the human brain. This was confirmed by Dr. Valerie Voon of University of Cambridge. Her study compared MRI pictures of active brains—one of an alcoholic, and the other of a porn addict. Appar-ently there is a part of our brain that functions as a reward mecha-nism. If an alcoholic watching television sees a commercial for liquor or cold beer, the reward mechanism in his brain lights up on the MRI. Intriguingly, the brain of a man addicted to porn reacts in exactly the same way when he sees images of illicit sexual contact.[7] This kind of neurological research has revealed that the effect of Internet porn on the human brain is just as potent, if not more so, than addictive drugs such as cocaine and heroin.

No wonder there are so many millions of users addicted to online porn!

I'm told that cocaine is a favorite drug for those craving to repeat a chemically induced high. Those who want "ecstasy" often choose cocaine. Heroin, on the other hand, has a relaxing effect. Both drugs develop chemical tolerance in the user, which means that each time you use them, you need higher quantities of the drug to achieve the same effect you felt earlier. While in my wayward youth I never used heavy drugs, I did choose the most abused drug in America, alcohol. All these drugs follow the same pattern.

A man says he's going to try something "just once," but the next time he needs just a bit more to get the same buzz he experienced before. And presto, he's addicted.

This reminds me of a trip I took to Alaska several years ago in the month of January. While I was in Anchorage, snow plows were everywhere, pushing snow off the roads and parking lots. Because the piles of snow can get so high, it's necessary for the city's speed limit signs to be taller than usual. And during the trip I'll never forget one sign that read, in essence, "Choose your lane carefully. You will be in the same rut for the next 125 miles."

Are you wondering why you can't seem to break free of the grip of pornography, even though you love Jesus and you're praying and giving and serving and *really* want to be free? It's because of the deep ruts you've created in your brain. Your addiction to pornography has created a chemical dependence in your brain, which, in turn, triggers a neurological reward system that goes off automatically, almost without noticing.

Think of your brain as a forest with trails and ruts worn down by people walking along the same paths, over and over again, day after day. These addictive pathways awaken a craving in your brain for novel porn content, such as taboo sexual acts, child porn, or sexual pleasure aroused by pain (either causing it or feeling it). Some addicts begin to hate themselves and want to inflict pain on others. Others have taken their own lives.

These brain ruts are more than you bargained for! You might have started out by saying, "I can turn it off any time I want to," but it hasn't quite turned out that way, has it? Have you ever heard someone say the same thing about smoking? About drinking?

"I'm not an alcoholic. I can quit any time I want to."

"I'm not addicted to cigarettes. After all, I smoke only two packs a day! I can stop any time I want to."

But again, it never seems to turn out that way, does it? At some point, we finally have to admit that yes, we have an addiction. And it's destroying us.

GUARD YOUR MIND

Given this chilling information, no wonder Solomon wrote in Proverbs 23:7, "For as [a man] thinks in his heart, so is he." And perhaps these days we have a greater appreciation for why he would warn us, "Keep your heart with all diligence, for out of it spring the issues of life" (Proverbs 4:23).

In light of pornography's alluring power, I can better appreciate this prayer from David: "Turn away my eyes from looking at worthless things, and revive me in Your way" (Psalm 119:37). And I see clearly the wisdom of Job: "I made a covenant with my eyes not to look lustfully at a young woman" (Job 31:1 NIV).

In a similar way, the writer of Hebrews advises us to "lay aside every weight, and the sin which so easily ensnares us" (Hebrews 12:1). The Greek word translated "ensnares" pictures a man, arms at his sides, with a vine tied around his body from his feet to his shoulders. In our day, I believe the vine has become a chain. If pornography has trapped you, you're chained, and it has stolen your liberty in Jesus Christ.

Pornographic movies, pictures, magazines, and other media depict naked people or illicit sex in a very open way in order to cause sexual arousal. The New Testament Greek word *porne* speaks of this kind of activity as sexual immorality. First Corinthians 6:9-11 teaches that individuals who stay in their sexual sin—who never repent of it and surrender to Christ—will not inherit the kingdom of God.

Satan masterfully seduces us to sin...and then violently accuses us of doing wrong. Who of us has not heard someone say, "I sinned this week, and God has done a number on me to make me feel guilty." That's a wrong perspective to have.

God wants to show you the road to recovery, redemption, and forgiveness, not make you feel guilty. When you feel overwhelmingly accused and even condemned, understand that Satan is at work. Let's get it straight: The devil is the accuser of the brethren, not God (see Revelation 12:10).

If you're hooked on Internet pornography, I know what you're thinking: *Hey, pastor, none of us is perfect.* While that's true, let me explain theologically what it means that none of us is perfect. This side of heaven, none of us will ever reach perfection, but we are to reach for it nonetheless. Paul wrote, "Not that I have already attained, or am already perfected; but I press on, that I may lay hold of that for which Christ Jesus has also laid hold of me" (Philippians 3:12).

The Christian life is one of pursuing Christlikeness. For as long as we remain on this earth, we will never become perfectly holy, but we're to pursue holiness. Paul didn't want to surrender to any sin that would hinder his spiritual progress. He took the same advice he had given to others in a different context: "Do not give the devil a foothold" (Ephesians 4:27 NIV).

Before we placed our faith in Jesus Christ, all of us habitually presented our bodies "as slaves of uncleanness, and of lawlessness leading to *more* lawlessness" (Romans 6:19). After the Holy Spirit comes to live in us, however, we are to present our bodies

> as slaves of righteousness for holiness. For when you were slaves of sin, you were free in regard to righteousness. What fruit did you have then in the things of which you are now ashamed? For the end of those things *is* death. But now having been set free from sin, and having become slaves of God, you have your fruit to holiness, and the end, everlasting life (Romans 6:19-22).

Once you turn away from pornography, you must replace it with something that you love even more. You can't break free in any other way. The problem with rejecting porn without replacing it with something you value more is that you've already proven you're a compulsive person. You *will* fill that void with something. It won't stay empty.

In Matthew 12, Jesus talked about a man who, after being delivered from a demon, failed to put something good in its place. Eventually seven other demons worse than the first returned with the original evil spirit to indwell that man. Jesus declared, "The final condition of that person is worse than the first" (verse 45 NIV).

"Oh, you're talking about self-reformation," someone says. "I just need to turn over a new leaf."

Sorry, but you're wrong. I guarantee you it won't be that easy! In fact, you're in for the battle of your life. I spoke to a leading psychologist about this issue, and he told me, "Don't go in with an easy punch, Pastor Johnny. Tell them the truth. At the absolute least, they're in for a one-year battle."

If you can't win this battle through self-reformation and self-effort, then how can you win?

SCHOOLS OF LOVE

We learn how to love God primarily by learning how to live life with others: *together*. In the late twentieth and early twenty-first centuries, we have seriously devalued the body of Christ. People say, "I love God, but I hate the institution of the church." But hold on a minute! Who instituted the church? Jesus Christ did. That's why we should love the church.

Faith in Jesus is always personal, but never private. A lot of people miss that truth! In the Bible, placing faith in Jesus is an individual matter, but not individualistic.

I left the pool room as a high school dropout, a teenage drunk addicted to both gambling and stealing. How did I get to where I am now? The family of God! Jesus started the church, and no believer on the face of the earth has grown or ever will grow to spiritual maturity without the help of the body of Christ, the family of God.

One evening recently I went out to dinner when a waitress approached our table. "God bless you, Pastor Johnny," she said. "I praise God for you."

I looked up to see a young lady. "Well, thank you," I replied, "but remind me why you're thanking the Lord for me?"

"Because three years ago I went into Hope Quest," she explained, mentioning a ministry of our church. "I was addicted, but we left the addiction there. My baby just turned three years old. God set me free!"

I like to refer to families as schools of love. In a family, we learn to love and to be loved. In a family, we encounter God's unconditional faithfulness to His people. In a family, we learn the very nature of God, that He is a gift-giving Lord who desires to bless the world by inviting people into His eternal community. In short, family is not only the place where we learn the content of our faith, but also where we encounter the love of God and get invited to live out the mission of God.

Most guys go to porn for physical and emotional comfort. The habit often develops in adolescence as a way of dealing with pain, sadness, loneliness, and a lack of emotional resources. As we've seen, simply taking porn away from an adult is not a long-term solution. The porn needs to be replaced with an even more powerful source of comfort.

The porn addict needs a safe, accepting, genuine relationship in which the man can be loved even in the midst of his sinful behavior. My favorite book in the Bible says, "Confess your trespasses to one to another, and pray one for another, that you may be healed" (James 5:16).

I myself am in an accountability group of five men. I love those men. I've grown to love them even more as we've gotten to know each other more deeply. We talk about struggles in our work, struggles in our homes, struggles in our personal lives. And then we pray for one another. We send texts to each other during the week, reminding one another that we're praying for each other. We journal our prayers and write down how God answers them.

Don't underestimate the benefit of community groups, Sunday school classes, and home Bible study groups! Godly relationships will give you the emotional support that porn cannot supply—and it all starts with your relationship with God.

Gene McConnell is a recovering porn addict who saw porn for the first time at age twelve (you can find his material at powertochange .com). His addiction cost him both his marriage and his ministry. He said, "The reason porn exists is that we live empty lives. The issue is intimacy, our greatest need."[8] Gene adds, "Take that [word *intimacy*] as into-me-see—you see my life and see who I am, and you love me. That's the greatest need, male and female. But [intimacy is] also our greatest fear—that if you know the real me, if you see my weaknesses, then you would abandon me."[9]

Someone will say, "I had a friend and I shared my struggles—and he's no longer my friend." No, you only *thought* you had a friend. A real friend will stick by you; an imposter will bail.

This is why God put us in a family. We need each other. We grow to love Jesus more because of the family God has put around us, encouraging us and teaching us and discipling us and maturing us. None of us, on our own, can get to where we need to be.

Could that be one reason why you're not doing well? Because you're trying to grow by yourself, outside the context of God's family?

COME CLEAN

I asked a psychologist friend to write a statement asking men to come clean. The statement says, "Please come out of hiding. Jesus stands ready and available to help and to heal. We are not here to make anyone feel condemned or stay hidden or private. I know you cannot control what others think and perceive, yet it is our desire for men trapped in any bondage to feel that they can risk coming out."

Secrecy and deception damage marital oneness, damage your relationship with God, damage your self-concept. They cause mistrust and short-circuit God's rule over your life.

I beg you, in Jesus's name, let today be the stopping point. See the stop sign in King Jesus's hand! Today is the day to take the off-ramp. Don't continue down this road! It only gets more dangerous. Without confessing your sin to a close, godly friend or to a counselor or a minister—someone who will hold you accountable and give you some practical steps to walk through—you have very little chance to ever come clean. The key to breaking free is to honor what James 5:16 says about confessing your trespasses to one another and praying for one another so that you may be healed.

The beauty of Christ is far better! It's not just a song. Jesus Christ really *is* altogether lovely. He is calling for you to repent and draw near to Him.

Why are you living a secret life? Why are you living in deception, which only leaves you dying on the inside? Stop choosing to live a lie.

I beg you in Jesus's name, come clean.

A Wisdom Call

While guys typically have no problem speaking about what they call drinking "recreationally" or "in moderation," they get very quiet indeed when their drinking habits start to shift. Did you know that the top two signs of problem drinking both involve secrecy? New Hope Recovery Center, an organization that helps addicts reclaim their lives, has developed a list of fourteen "signs" of a secret alcoholic. The top two are highly significant:

1. *Secret Drinking*—Drinking alone or before or after going out. Talk of "getting ready to go out" usually involves having drinks before going to an event. As alcohol use increases regularly, a person needs more to get the same effect. So the secret alcoholic often drinks before or after going to events involving alcohol to be at the same level as friends.

2. *Hiding*—Not only will secret alcoholics drink secretly, they will frequently have hiding places for alcohol. If you suspect someone of being a secret alcoholic, look for full or empty bottles or cans of alcohol in places where they normally aren't stored. Common hiding places are bathroom cabinets and shelves (often top shelves); in garages; in closets, clothes, bags, and suitcases; and in kitchen cabinets hidden behind other cans, jars, and boxes. Empty bottles and cans may be found under furniture and in cushions. Also look in outside garbage and recycling bins. Do you notice more bottles or cans than usual showing up in those places?[1]

Number 5 on this list is "making excuses to drink," number 7 is "increased isolation, loss of interest," and number 11 is "over-focus on alcohol." All of them speak in one way or another of keeping quiet about the truth.

While I recommend that Christian men drink no alcohol at all (we'll get to that shortly), you know you have a serious problem once you start hiding your alcohol use and taking care to speak of it as little as possible. In this chapter, I want to lay out what I believe is a sound biblical, medical, and philosophical view of the use and abuse of alcohol.

THE CONTROVERSY OVER DRINKING

Let me start by quoting what is, for me, the key verse on a believing man's use of alcohol. Proverbs 20:1 declares, "Wine is a mocker, strong drink is a brawler and whoever is led astray by it is not wise."

I fully realize that a lot of controversy surrounds the subject of a Christian's use of alcohol. Can it be used responsibly, moderately, and recreationally? Is it just a matter of Christian liberty? Some evangelicals within the Reformed community have lifted their glasses as a badge of Christian liberty. John MacArthur, a leading Bible teacher, has criticized this trend.

> If everything you know about Christian living came from blogs and websites in the young-and-restless district of the Reformed community, you might have the impression that beer is the principal symbol of Christian liberty. For some who self-identify as "Young, Restless, and Reformed," it seems beer is a more popular topic for study and discussion than the doctrine of predestination...It's clear that beer-loving passion is a prominent badge of identity for many in the YRR movement...Cast a disapproving eye...and you're likely to be swarmed by restless reformers denouncing legalism and wanting to debate whether it's a "sin" to drink wine.[2]

Many Christians would cite Galatians 5:13 in this regard: "For you, brethren, have been called to liberty; only do not use your liberty as an opportunity for the flesh, but through love serve one another." That verse doesn't close the debate, however. In fact, the very verse someone might use to claim liberty is the very verse I would use to say that no Christian should abuse his liberty by giving the flesh a golden opportunity to sin.

You need to know that I come from a family of alcohol abusers and that as I was growing up, I took the same foolish path. Some might believe that such a background would make it hard for me to form a fair and biblical view on the topic. But my genuine heart's desire is to treat this issue in a balanced way, with both compassion and conviction. Along those lines, I doubt I can say it any better than did a friend of mine, Josh Franklin:

> I will argue against drinking alcohol as a beverage and I will stand against the liquor industry with every fiber of my being. However, I know that there are those who disagree with me. They may feel that they have Scripture to support their moderate drinking. I do not have the right, nor does any other Christian, to look down my nose in a judgmental manner toward someone who is struggling to be free or for one reason or another does not feel that Scripture condemns the practice. In fact, the Scripture speaks strongly against pride and self-righteousness. Alcohol does not send a person to hell. It's not what we'd call a top-tier doctrine of our faith and practice as believers. So I do not look down on those individuals who have taken an honest, unbiased look at the issues surrounding alcohol and hold a different view.[3]

I am not a teetotaler because I am a legalist. I am a teetotaler because I believe in my heart that God set me free from alcohol. I'm also a teetotaler because I refuse to encourage any man, in any way, to make himself a prisoner of strong drink.

THE BATTLE TO DRINK

Many godly men battle with whether Christians ought to drink.

They're living for Jesus. They love God, and they don't want to do anything improper.

Recently a man left my office saying, "I want you to know I'm leaving here and going to get a cold beer. I'm going to sit down and drink it to the glory of God." I thought, *Okay, see you.* People frequently challenge my position, and that's fine by me.

Not long ago I was at a restaurant with a young man I'm mentoring. The bartender soon brought over a beer and sat it down in front of me. "This is a gift for you, Mr. Hunt," he said, "from somebody who cares a great deal for you."

"No thank you, sir," I answered. "I appreciate it, but you can take it back."

"But it's free," he replied.

In the back of my mind I thought, *No, for a lot people it's not free. It cost them their marriage. It cost them their job. It cost them their home.*

Did you know that from 2001 to 2007, the alcoholic beverage industry spent $6.6 billion on television advertising? In 2007 alone, more than 40 percent of youth exposure to alcohol occurred during programs viewed by youth.[4]

What really concerns me is that the median age at which children begin drinking is about 14 years of age. And "people who reported starting to drink before the age of 15 were four more times likely to also report meeting the criteria for alcohol dependence in their lives."[5]

We're told that by age 18, approximately 60 percent of teens have had at least one drink. And in 2015, 7.7 million individuals between the ages of 12-20 said they had drank alcohol in the previous month.[6]

Why should Christian leaders remain silent on this issue when our young people are being put at risk? Is it not our responsibility, at home and at church, to give a biblical basis for Christian behavior, so that we can fortify and equip our young people for a long and fruitful life?

Teenage drinkers are more likely to engage in premarital sex. Why? Because alcohol relaxes one's morals. And studies have shown that youth who drink alcohol at any level are definitely more likely to use an illicit drug than those who have never taken a drink.

It's a wisdom call.

I have to ask myself how, as a spiritual leader who's trying to make a difference for God and good in this nation, I could ever lead the way in encouraging people to drink alcohol.

Danny Akin, president of Southeastern Baptist Theological Seminary, said, "Today there are more than 40 million problem drinkers in America. Alcohol is the number one drug problem among teenagers. One in three American families suspects that one or more family members are having a drinking problem."[7]

I myself have a close relative with whom I find it hard to carry on a coherent conversation. Why? Because most of the time he is under the influence.

BLOOD ALCOHOL LEVELS

May I tell you what most concerns me as a Christian leader? That's easy: Blood alcohol concentration.

Before I became a Christian, I borrowed my sister's car to go on a date. I'd been drinking that night, and after I took my date home, I got into some trouble. To make a long story short, I totaled my sister's automobile.

I've been paying for it ever since.

That night, the arresting police officer wrote me a DUI (driving under the influence). I spent the night in the New Hanover County Jail. The next morning, my mother came to get me out. Back in those days, if you blew a breathalyzer test of .07 or more, you were guilty of driving under the influence. Today, it's .08 or higher.

May I ask a question? Suppose you believe in drinking moderately and recreationally, and you believe you're drinking responsibly. Imagine that one night you go out with your buddies, who keep pushing one drink after another in front of you. On the drive home, you get stopped because you wander a little over the center line on the road. The police write you up as DUI, which from a legal standpoint means you were driving drunk.

What should a church do with a deacon, pastor, or staff member who winds up in the public records slapped with this note: "Apprehended while driving under the influence"?

It's a wisdom call.

How does even a little alcohol affect the human body? Let's consider a blood alcohol level of from .01 to .05. What happens when any person has a glass of wine, a twelve-ounce can of beer, or a quarter ounce of the hard stuff, such as whiskey or vodka?

Some individuals immediately suffer a significant loss of judgment and coordination. Their thinking gets dulled, resulting in changes of mood and behavior. If someone who weighs 129 pounds or less downs a twelve-ounce beer, four ounces of wine, or a quarter ounce of 80 proof liquor, he will register a blood alcohol level of from .05 to .08—teetering right on the legal line. Most women will blow into that breathalyzer and wind up in jail.

What other effects will that small amount of alcohol have? The individual's walking, speech, and hand movements may become clumsy. Blurred or split tunnel vision may occur. The chance of getting in an accident increases by up to 300 percent.

It's a wisdom call.

WHO HAS WOE?

Solomon, the wisest man who ever lived, asked, "Who has woe? Who has sorrow? Who has contention? Who has complaints? Who has wounds without cause? Who has redness of eyes?" And then he answered his own question: "Those who linger long at the wine" (Proverbs 23:29-30). When Solomon spoke of "woe" and "sorrow," he meant that alcohol can lead to a mountain of emotional problems. "Contentions" and "complaints" refer to a host of social problems. "Wounds" and "redness of eyes" point to physical problems.

Proverbs 23:35 speaks from the perspective of a man who's had a few too many: "They have struck me but I was not hurt; they have beaten me, but I did not feel it. When shall I awake, that I may seek another drink?"

Have you considered that the person who drinks with you may

become the next alcoholic? You may be helping to create yet another addict. In the end, the Bible says that alcohol bites like a serpent and stings like a viper (Proverbs 23:32). As Pastor James Merritt says, "It is impossible to be bitten by a snake that you never play with."[8]

All of this leads to the following questions: Should you drink or not? Is it wrong? Is it right? The law says it's okay, but the law also says abortion is okay and that same-sex marriage is okay. So do you let man-made laws be your guide?

Here's the bottom line: Like it or not, you may *already* be categorized by the medical community as a social alcoholic. Every night, you want a beer. Every night, you want wine. You never think about dinner without having an alcoholic beverage. For you, it's become a regular part of your evening routine.

Former President George W. Bush quit drinking at age forty. His wife, Laura, had challenged him to stop drinking, but nothing really changed until after she asked him a troubling question. She asked him if he could remember the last day he *hadn't* had a drink. That's when George began to realize he had to make a choice between alcohol or God. Among the things that helped George to stop drinking were "a meeting with evangelist Billy Graham and regularly attending Bible study."[9]

WHAT IS STRONG DRINK?

I have wondered if we really understand what the Bible has in view when it refers to strong drink, or what it means when it tells us not to be led astray by it. The fact is, the wine that people drank in Bible days was far different from the way wine is made today.

In ancient times, fermented beverages contained no alcohol. People drank nonalcoholic wine, to which they sometimes added other ingredients, such as figs. Alcohol is produced only when some mechanical process of distillation interferes with the normal process of fermentation. The ancient Hebrews would have referred to our wine and beer as strong drink.

I can't tell you how many times I've heard someone say, "I don't think drinking wine is wrong. Didn't Jesus turn water into wine? Didn't the early church use wine to celebrate the Lord's Supper? Didn't Jesus say He'd drink wine once more with His disciples at the end of the age?"

All of that is true—but the wine Jesus drank, and will drink again one day, was and will be nothing like the wine we know today. That's an apples-to-oranges comparison. Jesus was not in the liquor business. New Testament scholar Dr. Robert Stein researched the wine drinking of the ancient world, scouring both Jewish sources and the Bible. He made a fascinating discovery about the wine of the Bible era as compared to the wine of today. The wine back then bore little resemblance to today's product.[10]

In fact, our wine is actually the "strong drink" of the Bible—and every time strong drink gets mentioned in Scripture, it's condemned. Never once is it condoned. The wine, beer, and alcoholic beverages of our day are not remotely equivalent to the wine of the first century. Rather, they all fit into the strong drink category, which the Bible universally condemns.

People of the first century typically mixed wine with water— normally one part of wine to three or four parts of water. In other words, what the Bible calls wine was essentially purified water. In the ancient world, plain water was unsafe to drink. People made it safe by boiling it, filtering it, or by the safest and easiest method, by mixing it with wine (which killed the germs present in the water).

Our problem today is that wine, beer, and other fermented beverages have high alcohol content. Such high concentrations of alcohol didn't become more widespread until the Middle Ages, when the Arabs invented distillation. So what we now call liquor, the Bible calls strong drink. The 20 percent alcohol-fortified wines we have today were simply unknown in Bible times.

You may choose to disagree with me, but please do not cite the wine of the New Testament era as your argument for consuming strong drink in this generation. The two are clearly not the same thing. Dr. Stein noted that one would have to drink twenty-two glasses of first-century wine in order to consume the same amount of alcohol we get in only two martinis.[11]

Fox movie executives once invited Janet and me, at their expense, to fly to Los Angeles. They wanted us to watch the newest movie in the Chronicles of Narnia series. Forty other pastors joined us. Fox took us to a basketball game and gave us the use of the owners' suite, which had an open bar. I may be wrong, but of all the preachers there, I think just three of us were teetotalers. The other pastors were drinking eighteen- and twenty-four-ounce beers, which would put every one of them above the legal definition of drunkenness. They were drinking straight liquor. I used to drink, so I know the drill.

When we got back on the bus, *wow*! A very strong aroma of alcohol filled our nostrils. It's good that our hosts had designated someone to drive us back to the hotel.

I know pastors who would stand a bottle of beer right next to a Bible and say, "There's nothing in this book that tells us drinking is wrong." I would say to them, "The beer you're using as a prop is not even mentioned in the Bible, except when it's condemned as strong drink." Again, you simply cannot compare the wine of the first century with the wine of today.

Norman Geisler, a wonderful conservative Bible scholar, said, "Christians ought not to drink wine, beer or other alcoholic beverages for they are actually strong drink and forbidden in Scripture. Even ancient pagans did not drink what Christians drink today."[12]

Danny Akin wrote, "It is true Jesus drank wine, and I am sure I would have had I lived in the first century. However, there is no evidence at all that he ever partook of 'strong drink.'" Danny went on to cite Bob Stein, who said, "[I]t is possible to become intoxicated from wine mixed with three parts of water, but one's drinking would probably affect the bladder long before it affected the mind." Danny then said,

> It should also be noted that children would have drank this diluted mixture of water and wine, and it is impossible to imagine godly parents giving their children a drink that could get them drunk…It again seems clear that there is no one-to-one correspondence with first century wine and twenty-first century distilled intoxication liquor.

Concerning the latter, I believe the Lord Jesus Christ would have no part.[13]

THE IMPACT OF ALCOHOL

Even if Scripture were silent on this issue, the horrific impact of alcohol on today's society would prompt me to publicly condemn its use. I would challenge every Christian man with the words of Romans 14:21: "It is good neither to eat meat nor drink wine nor do anything by which your brother stumbles or is offended or is made weak."

Every year, some 1,825 college students die from alcohol-related unintentional injuries, including car crashes.[14] That's four jumbo jetliners packed with college students. What would happen to the aircraft manufacturer if, in a single year, four of its jetliners crashed and killed everyone on board?

We know that a lot of the discipline-related issues on college campuses today are related to alcohol. For example, "about 696,000 students between the ages of 18 and 24 are assaulted by another student who has been drinking," and "about 97,000 students between the ages of 18 and 24 report experiencing alcohol-related sexual assault or date rape."[15] Alcohol clearly has a damaging influence. Shakespeare put it this way: "Oh God, that men would put an enemy in their mouth to steal away their brain."

And what about your influence on others? In your home, at work, at school, you can influence others for good or for ill. I speak at a lot of events. I spoke recently to 1,200 business people at High Point University in North Carolina. Do you know why they asked me to come? They wanted me to tell my personal story, which I call "From the Pool Room to the Pulpit." I never worry at these events about what they might serve for beverages. I stay with my agenda of telling the story of how Jesus Christ changed my life and delivered me from a drunkard's fate.

Adrian Rogers once shared about the time when, while he pastored a church in Fort Pierce, Florida, he had an artist help him recreate a slick advertisement extolling "the finest product of the brewer's art"—but with a little twist. Instead of portraying the "finest product," he depicted the "finished product" of the brewer's art: a disheveled man in an alley, with a broken bottle, garbage cans by his side, and a big rat running past him. This appeared on a billboard in the church's parking lot.

Afterward, Adrian got a call from a beer distributor who asked to meet with him. The executive was offended, and asked him to take the sign down. Adrian said he would do it only if the distributor took down all his signs.[16]

Think about it: A liquor industry executive tried to stop one pastor from posting a single billboard to warn his congregation of the dangers of alcohol, when that same industry spends billions in advertising to tell Americans they ought to drink. Amazing!

DON'T DRINK

There's a collection of short statements you may have heard before that address the fact wine is a deceiver. Here's an excerpt:

> We drank for happiness and became unhappy.
>
> We drank for joy and became miserable.
>
> We drank for sociability and became argumentative.
>
> We drank for sophistication and become obnoxious.
>
> We drank for friendship and made enemies.[17]

That last line reminds me of an incident that someone told me about, which took place at an Atlanta Braves baseball game. Two guys seated in front of him seemed to be the best of buds. They were slapping each other on the back, having a great time. And then they started downing a good number of beers. After a while, they both got pretty tanked and ended up getting into a fight. Isn't that amazing? Had they remained sober, they probably never would have taken a swing at each other.

The statements continue:

We drank for sleep and woke up tired.

We drank for strength and became weak.

We drank for relaxation and got the shakes.

We drank for courage and became afraid.

We drank for confidence and became doubtful.

We drank to make conversation and our speech became
slurred.

We drank to feel heavenly and ended up feeling like hell.

We drank to forget and became forever haunted.

We drank for freedom and became slaves.

We drank to erase problems and saw them multiply.

We drank to cope with life and invited death.[18]

Do you know what I think is best advice when it comes to drinking?
Don't drink.

QUESTIONS TO CONSIDER

As I've said, I was converted from a life of alcohol abuse. By the
grace of God, I and countless others have been delivered and made
strong. One of our deacons stopped me one day as I walking through
a hallway at our church. "My life never took on meaning," he said,
"until I was able to lay the bottle aside and to embrace Jesus Christ as
my Lord and Savior."

You may believe you drink responsibly. You may say you drink in
moderation. You may believe that you're at liberty to do so and therefore you disagree with my stance.

Do me a favor, will you? Do all the research you can, and when you
finish, send me the proof that what you're drinking today is equivalent
to what Jesus drank in the first century.

It would be a lot easier for me to leave this topic alone and make
every man feel comfortable in his "moderation," but let me ask one

final set of questions. In your social drinking, have you ever had one drink too many? And if you have, is that alcoholism? Do you know an alcoholic? Have you ever met an alcoholic? Are you concerned about alcoholics? Would you want to contribute to an industry that has helped to ruin countless lives over the centuries?

I thank God for every father who has taken a stand to lead his children to be total abstainers. And I pray in Jesus's name that all of us would live for Jesus first, and then for others.

At the end of the day, I choose to be a teetotaler. I've made that choice for the last forty-five years, after nine dismal years of abusing alcohol. I'm not ashamed to talk about it.

By any chance, are you hesitant to speak about your own use of alcohol?

6

THE PRESSURE
OF PROVIDING

Many men today are under great pressure to live up to expectations about caring adequately for their families. According to one article, even guys not yet married feel a "deep-seated need to be competent and successful, coupled by the conscious conviction that society is always watching and judging their performance."[1]

One person mentioned in the article, a twenty-eight-year-old addiction counselor working on a graduate degree in psychology, declared, "Men are under a lot of pressure to perform and we feel that everyone is watching and judging us: where does he work? Where do his kids attend school? What does the wife look like? What does he drive? We are always thinking, 'How am I doing? What's my score?' Granted we pressure ourselves enough without external pressure, but the quickest way to make a man feel inadequate is to constantly remind him that his performance isn't good enough; whether it's at being a father, husband, lover, employee, business man, at fixing the TV...whatever."[2]

The writer concluded, "No matter how that initial question was asked, no matter what the topic on the table was, everything always led back to this articulation...the very core of every man's identity is the desire and profound burden to provide. This is how he says 'I love you.'"[3]

I believe that's right on the money. At the core of every man's identity is the desire to provide well for his family. Without question this pressure can snowball into something utterly overwhelming.

WHO, ME?

While a lot of men stagger under the weight of providing for their families and trying to meet all the expectations that others place on them, most of the men I know rarely, if ever, talk about it. They may feel inadequate, they may screw up, they may dislike the house they live in or disapprove of the schools their kids attend, but rarely will they admit to anyone, "I'm having a hard time providing for my family."

Which leads me to ask this: When did *you* last hear any of your buddies make such an admission? Have any of your friends ever said that?

I didn't think so.

Guys want to be good providers. It's in their DNA. From the very beginning, way back in the Garden of Eden, God gave man a job. We're told that "the Lord God took the man and put him in the garden of Eden to tend and keep it" (Genesis 2:15). To this day, men have a powerful, divinely implanted urge deep within them to work hard and take care of their families.

It would be enough of a challenge if this mandate to provide involved only employment and finances. Trying to make enough money to take care of one's family has pushed men to the limit throughout history, and we're no exception today. But modern life has thrown a number of additional elements into the mix.

For one thing, never before in history has the job landscape changed so continuously, rapidly, thoroughly, and unexpectedly. Advances in technology fuel the development and demolition of entire industries almost overnight. In fact, I have a hard time thinking of *any* industry in the past few decades that has avoided rapid and significant change. Higher education? No. Publishing? Nope. Medicine? No. The music or film industry? No. Manufacturing? No. Accounting? No. How about church ministry? Surely that looks pretty much the same as it did twenty or thirty years ago? Don't make me laugh.

With all of the radical transformations and unforeseen changes in the way the world works, men today often wonder if the job they have now will even exist in a few years. In mid-2017, *nine* large US retail chains filed for Chapter 11 bankruptcy, and nearly 90,000 retail workers had lost their jobs since the previous October.[4] "The disruption is just unfolding," said Mark Cohen, a former CEO of Sears Canada who currently directs retail studies at Columbia Business School. "I think the number of store closings will continue at an accelerated pace right through this year into next year."[5] Losing a job or wondering whether you'll still have your job in six months can take its own toll, beyond the pressure of actually making enough money to sustain your family.

But providing for your family implies a lot more than economics. Even the dictionary tells us that *provide* can mean "to furnish, supply, or equip," as well as "to take measures with due foresight." A man who wants to provide for his household has to make sure that he equips his family to thrive in all areas of life, wherever the Lord has planted them—and that takes a certain amount of planning and foresight. It also raises a truckload of questions.

What about the spiritual needs of a man's family? If God considers a man the spiritual head of his home, what does that involve? Does he need to teach his children how to pray? How to read and study the Bible? How does he help lead them to a saving knowledge of Jesus Christ? What does it look like for him to lead his wife in spiritual matters? What if she's a better thinker, speaker, or leader than he is? How could that change the dynamics of his home? What is his responsibility to the church that the family attends? Do they attend only on Sunday, and that's it? Does he get involved in teaching a class, attending a class, or cleaning up after a class? Is he giving his kids opportunities to be involved with other kids at church? How does he integrate his home life with his family's church life?

How does a man provide for the disciplinary needs of his home? How can he make sure that he and his wife are on the same page when they need to dole out discipline? What does that discipline look like? Does the man have to be the main disciplinarian? If he's not, how can he still lead in this area? How can he be sure that his discipline is consistent, fair, and positive?

What happens when the house needs repairs, or an appliance or some piece of equipment goes on the fritz, or the trees need trimming?

Does he have to be the "fix-it" man for it all? What if he's not particularly handy, but doesn't have the cash required to keep up with maintenance? How does he provide for his family to make sure that the home environment remains safe, attractive, and healthy?

When his wife suffers some personal setback and needs significant emotional support, what can he do to help? How can he equip his kids to make it through the trials of junior high or middle school? When his kids get old enough to start dating, how will he handle *that* emotional roller coaster? Is he prepared to teach his son about the birds and the bees? How can he provide the emotional stability his family needs through both thick and thin?

If he's no longer the Greek god he (thinks he) once was, where can he find the time to get back in shape physically? Can he ride a bike, join a gym, take up jogging, play some recreational league ball? How can he encourage his whole family to stay in good physical shape? Does he know who's scheduled for a doctor's or dentist's appointment, and when? Does he work with his wife to provide healthy, nutritious food for the family, or does he tend to fall back on fast food?

And on and on it goes.

The sobering reality is that providing for one's family covers an enormous amount of rugged territory. When you include the expectations (reasonable and otherwise) of others, and then factor in the probability that multitudes of observers are taking careful note of what happens under your roof (at least, as much as they can see through the windows), it can all add up to a mountain of *PRESSURE*.

WHERE DO YOU WIN...OR WILT?

I know of some guys who handle family financial pressures with ease, but who wilt at the spiritual leadership requirements of the job. Others manage to keep themselves and the members of their family in tip-top physical shape, but run away whenever someone comes to them with an emotional need. What kind of pressures do you deal with as you provide for your family?

Where do you think you excel as a provider?

Where do you struggle?

Where do you wish you had a little help in improving some aspect of your performance as the family provider?

Most of all, to whom do you go when you need to talk about the pressures of providing? Who can you call on to help you process the burden you feel? And just as important, are *you* the kind of friend who other men can depend on to give prayerful attention and a sympathetic ear?

We all have times when it feels as though everything we've worked for and labored to create might come crashing down upon our heads. We feel tired, weary, discouraged, disappointed, and maybe more than a little frightened—although we wouldn't dream of telling anyone any of that.

But why not? How could it hurt to let someone else know the enormous pressure you feel? Wouldn't it actually be more beneficial to speak up to someone you can trust?

In the Bible, we meet a couple of men who, many centuries ago, made the courageous choice to admit their own "I'm at the end of my rope" moment. At more than one time in my life, their words have given me much-needed hope and encouragement in the middle of crushing pressure.

RAISING THE DEAD

I think all of us need periodic reminders that the Christian life is a battleground, not a playground. We ought to expect trouble, even while continuing to anticipate that God will do great things for us and in us.

If you feel under extreme pressure because of your responsibilities as a provider, recognize that others have experienced the same thing long before you did. Life has a way of putting us in a vise and squeezing. No less than the apostle Paul once wrote to some dear friends, "We do not want you to be ignorant, brethren, of our trouble which came to us in Asia: that we were burdened beyond measure, above strength, so that we despaired even of life. Yes, we had the sentence of death in ourselves" (2 Corinthians 1:8-9 NIV).

You might feel, right at this moment, under "the sentence of death." The pressure may have mounted to the point where you can't see how you could take one step more. The burden you feel, just as Paul described it so long ago, is far beyond your ability to endure.

So what do you do? You could follow the apostle's example. Do you realize that the only reason we can read his words in 2 Corinthians 1:8-9 is that he made the choice to tell others about his heavy burden? He didn't keep it to himself. Nor did he downplay or superspiritualize his plight. He didn't say, "Things looked bad for us, brothers, real bad, but praise the Lord, we just claimed the victory in Jesus's name and He put us on the mountaintop." No, Paul admitted the truth, in all its harshness. He told his friends that troubles had burdened him "beyond measure." The pressures grew so enormous that the apostle "despaired of life," even to such a degree that he "had the sentence of death" upon him. Now *that's* serious.

If the pressure is crushing you, then why not follow Paul's example and tell some close friends about it? Let them know how you feel. Don't hold back. Don't whitewash your fears or mask your anxiety. Paul told his friends he thought he was going to die. He didn't appear to care if any of them might think, *Whoa, Bud, you need to get a grip.* He had no need to convince them he was some superman because he knew he wasn't. He was forthright and told it like it was.

I'm glad Paul didn't stop there. He didn't merely dump all his fears and anxieties on his friends and then say, on his way out the door, "Thanks a lot, guys." He had the wisdom to put his terrible troubles in context. God gave him the insight to see that, even in those desperately dark hours, the Lord had a purpose and a design. Paul went on to tell his friends, "This happened that we might not rely on ourselves but on God, who raises the dead" (verse 9 NIV).

Whenever you find yourself under the massive pressure that often accompanies your responsibility to provide, God means for you to look up. You can't rely on yourself. How could you? You might feel at death's doorstep, one foot from the grave—and the only One qualified to raise the dead is God.

A little later in his letter, Paul updated his friends on his situation. While the Lord had rescued him from the despair that not long before had clawed at his heels, the apostle hadn't yet broken out into rainbows and sunbeams. While the pressure had abated some, it hadn't disappeared. And Paul told the truth about that too: "We are hard-pressed on every side, yet not crushed," he wrote. "We are perplexed, but not in despair; persecuted, but not forsaken; struck down, but not destroyed" (2 Corinthians 4:8-9). Note that all those verbs appear in the present tense: Paul *is* hard-pressed, he *is* perplexed, he *is* persecuted, he *is* struck down. He no longer feels at death's door, but he's still under significant pressure.

I believe it is the work of the Holy Spirit to bring us to our knees when we have a pressing need. The supply we receive from our loving Father may not be that for which we petitioned Him, but in His own way, He will bring us through the pressure. There may be a more urgent need we have that we did not comprehend. He will supply according to *that* need.

A WINESKIN IN SMOKE

Long before Paul's day, another man of God felt stretched and torn under a very different set of circumstances. Although he had studied God's Word faithfully and put his trust in the Lord, vicious enemies had attacked him and persecuted him without cause. Despite many prayers for deliverance, the pressure kept building, unrelentingly, until he called himself "a wineskin in smoke" (Psalm 119:83).

In ancient times, people used animal skins to make containers that held water and wine. Over time, as these containers were exposed to the smoke and heat of cooking fires in the home's hearth, they would dry up and shrivel. Once this happened, the containers were useless. The dry, cracked skins could no longer serve their function, and their owners would throw them out as worthless.

What a dismal self-portrait the psalmist painted! He saw himself as drawn, stretched thin, dry, cracked, and useless. He was spent, worn out, consumed. He had lost all influence. He felt tossed aside and forgotten. *Not even God remembers me,* he may have thought.

Have you ever felt like a wineskin in smoke? Maybe the pressures of providing for your family have stretched you paper-thin. Maybe you feel dry, cracked, worn out, and useless. Maybe you feel like some guys I met not too long ago.

One evening I had dinner with three young couples. As the night wore on, we began to talk about money. Each of the three couples had similar stories regarding their finances. They had all gotten deeper and deeper into debt.

As we discussed the difficult issues brought on by their indebtedness, all the couples expressed eerily similar regrets. Without exception, each of them shared a sense of calling, but believed that their bad decisions concerning money had left them on the edge of catastrophe. One husband said, "I'd be in ministry today if it were not for my debt."

As we continued to talk, I couldn't help but notice the obvious readiness and eagerness of the wives to discuss this sensitive issue. They took the lead. By contrast, all the men held back and seemed reluctant to join the conversation. Only as our discussion progressed did they finally begin to chime in.

I believe the men's reluctance reflected their deep pain as the families' chief breadwinners. No doubt they felt the heavier part of the load for their financial predicament. The men clearly felt stretched, almost useless. It wouldn't surprise me to learn that one or more of them had already begun edging toward depression.

I don't make this connection lightly. As I draft this chapter, I am seeking to encourage the wife of a very discouraged man. After losing his job and failing to find another one, he has fallen into depression. He believes he has lost the ability to provide for his family, and it's killing him. He feels like a wineskin in smoke. His wife recently listed for me the words and phrases she most often hears from him these days: "useless," "unable to cope," "failure," and "I've let my family down."

I'm grateful that, like the apostle Paul, the writer of Psalm 119 didn't stop with the gloomy description of his dark, pressure-filled life. It encourages me to note that the psalmist—again, like Paul—felt no shame in telling others of his desperate situation. He admitted, as did Paul, that death was on his mind: "They almost made an end of me on earth" (verse 87). Yet again, like Paul, he held on to that idea of "almost."

Yes, the hour was urgent, the crisis was clear, the need was great. The situation had become critical, and the sand in the hourglass read, "Almost exhausted." The man hovered on the brink of disaster. He needed rescue of body and revival of spirit.

But he was not without hope. We never are.

You never are.

Still, he had questions, as you no doubt do too. First, he asked God, "When will You comfort me?" (verse 82). This is the natural response of suffering people. For most of us, it is difficult to wait for the things we *can* see—a traffic jam to end, a checkout line to speed up, a temporary illness to pass. But it is far more difficult to wait for our unseen Lord to work out His will.

I wonder, though, if sometimes we suffer unnecessarily. How often do we suffer a long time under the pressure of providing because we want God to take care of our problem *directly*, without resorting to the help of others around us? Like the psalmist, our soul "faints" for God's salvation (verse 81)—but in our case, it's often because we don't want to have to admit our predicament to anyone else.

What if, however, other followers of Jesus *are* God's solution to your problem? What if the Lord wants to give you relief through someone else? And what if He wants to start giving you that relief only as you reach out to a trusted friend to talk about the unbearable pressure you're feeling?

"Blessed be the God and Father of our Lord Jesus Christ, the Father of mercies and God of all comfort," Paul wrote, "who comforts us in all our tribulation, *that we may be able to comfort those who are in any trouble*, with the comfort with which we ourselves are comforted by God" (2 Corinthians 1:3-4; emphasis added). God has placed us within a church body so that one suffering member in need of comfort can find relief and comfort through another member. In that way, it is God who "comforts us in all our tribulation." *God* ministers to us and delivers His comfort *through* others.

But to receive that kind of comfort, you have to let someone know you need it. Are you willing to do that? Are you willing to make known to a fellow brother that which you have left unspoken?

Difficulties like this can often go from bad to worse. In Psalm 119, by verse 84 the psalmist was asking, "How many are the days of Your servant?" In other words, "I don't think I'm long for this world, Lord. Couldn't You hurry it up a bit? How much longer can I take this? My days are slipping away, and yet my prayers remain unanswered." These are not, by the way, questions of unbelief. These are the questions of suffering saints. We all go through what we consider "strange delays" in God's handling of tough situations. We don't like them. They make no sense to us. They feel unfair, even cruel.

We need to remember that they don't last forever.

As with Job, and also here with the psalmist, God draws a line in the sand—a line beyond which persecutors cannot go. The psalmist said his enemies "almost" made an end of him, and God's "almost" is an impenetrable barrier that no enemy can breach.

You probably don't have the kinds of enemies the psalmist had, but the pressures that burden you are still enemies of one kind or another. God says "almost" to those enemies too. They cannot defeat you unless you attempt to tackle them on your own. It takes a band of brothers to help you push back and stand strong. Who's in your band?

You need other guys to help you. God wants to use them to revive your soul and energize your spirit. I know you want to obey the Lord, but I also know you don't have the strength to do it on your own. You need God to revive you, to breathe into you His life-giving, life-transforming power. You need a fresh touch of God's grace to strengthen you. And it's very likely that God wants to use other men to bring you to that place of renewed strength and power.

TALK TO HIM

In 1979, when the rulers of communist China decided to limit the size of that nation's families (the infamous "one-child policy"), no one in the government clearly foresaw the problems the policy would create. Today, those difficulties have become evident.

The first generation of children reared under the one-child policy have been coming of age. More often than not, these young adults live under extraordinary pressure. Why? Because as young men and women who themselves are parents of just one child, they also must now take care of two sets of aging parents. According to an article in a Chinese publication, observers have called this the "4-2-1" family structure, and it's causing almost unbelievable angst in modern China.[6] More than six million Chinese parents received a one-child certificate back in 1979, and now millions of their one-child children are finding themselves in what for many of them feels like an impossible situation.

The article went on to tell the story of a Mr. Wang and his wife, who feel extraordinary pressure to provide for their extended family. "They feel extremely tired because they are under the mental pressure of supporting their aging parents and have to face the realistic difficulties in raising their child," said the article. "Like Mr. Wang, many of those who are the only child in their family have to face the issue of supporting their parents. They are worried that they can neither afford to raise their child nor support their parents."[7]

While Americans have never had to live under such an unbiblical policy, millions of men do live under the daily, unrelenting pressure of providing well for their families. Reading a chapter like this one will not relieve them of that pressure, but I hope that by now, you realize what you need to do to reduce the pressure enough that you gain a new sense of hope.

And what is it you need to do? Proverbs 18:24 says, "There is a friend who sticks closer than a brother" (Proverbs 18:24). Find that friend, and talk to him.

I Need a
Money Miracle

Some time ago the pastor of a large Midwestern church decided to do a series of talks on finances. Several members and regular attenders of his church had come to him privately, asking for some fiscal counseling to help them get back on track with their unhealthy spending habits. He began his first presentation one Sunday morning by saying something like this:

"I'd like to ask a single question of every person in this auditorium. But before I ask it, I'd like everyone here to close your eyes. Please shut your eyes for just a moment, and don't look around. Thank you so much. Now here's the question: How many of you present this morning need a financial miracle? Whether you need a financial miracle in your home or in your business, please raise your hand."

He expected maybe a dozen hands to go up. He never imagined the response he would get: *Three-quarters* of the people raised their hands. The sea of hands shocked him. And it stunned him even more that he got virtually the same result in all three of that Sunday morning's services.

Had you been in the audience that morning, how would you have responded? Would your hand have shot up?

FINANCES OUT OF CONTROL

Although America is by far the richest nation on the planet, a large percentage of us lack sound financial habits. Consider, for example, that as of June 2017, the estimated average US household savings rate stood at only 5.25 percent. Compare that figure with the savings rate in nations such as Germany and Sweden, which, during the same period, stood at 10 percent or more.[1] We Americans may have more money than others around the world, but a shocking percentage of us don't spend it wisely. No wonder so many of us are in real financial trouble!

And yet we keep our mouths shut about it.

We don't want anyone to know that we teeter every month on the brink of economic ruin. We may tell our buddies about the new car we've bought, or the great vacation we have planned, or the big grill we ordered, or the sleek boat we have our eyes on—but we remain silent about the very real possibility that the repo man might show up at our doorstep any evening now.

I'm not suggesting that we broadcast to all comers about our money troubles. But neither does it help us to keep quiet about our problem and pretend as though it doesn't exist. Wisdom insists that we absolutely *have* to get a handle on our use of money. That's extremely unlikely to happen, however, if we don't admit where we are financially and then seek some wise counsel from informed sources who can help us to get back on a sound financial footing.

In this chapter, I'd like for us to look at what the Bible has to say about some of our most common money mistakes. I also want to tap into the wisdom of some godly financial advisors whose counsel I know has enabled many men to move from deep anxiety over their economic situation to strong confidence. And I'll also tell a number of real-life stories that put flesh on the abstract idea of mastering financial responsibility.

LIVING IN A CREDIT-CRAZY CULTURE

In general, most of us get into financial trouble simply because we don't keep a close watch on how much money we have coming in or going out. We live in a credit-crazy culture in which we constantly get bombarded with messages that urge us to buy what we "deserve" *right now*, whether or not we have the funds. "Hey, we'll give you a loan!

Don't worry about how much it costs—we'll make the monthly payments easy for you."

And before we know it, we find ourselves deep in debt. We wake up in the middle of the night, full of anxiety that we can't make our mortgage payment this month. We stop saving, we stop giving to the Lord through our church, we abandon important things like life insurance or even health insurance. And when an emergency hits—and life has a way of making sure we all face emergencies at the most inopportune times—we crumble.

MOST COMMON MONEY MISTAKES

Consider just ten of the most common money mistakes that Americans tend to make. Do you recognize yourself or your family in any of the ten?

1. Spending too much on unnecessary items

Do you realize that spending just $25 per week dining out adds up to $1,300 a year? How often do you buy a morning coffee at the neighborhood coffee shop rather than brewing your own? Do you buy premium gas when your vehicle doesn't need it? How often do you make impulse purchases at the grocery store or department store? What kind of never-ending payments do you have, such as expensive smartphone plans, deluxe cable TV subscriptions, video games, etc.?

2. Lack of a household budget

Failing to plan is planning to fail. How much do you spend every month on food, clothes, utilities, mortgage, insurance, eating out, phone, broadband, gasoline, medical, dental, etc.? If you don't know, almost certainly you're spending too much. Do you keep a running track of all your expenses? Or do you just use your debit card to pay for everything from a single "pot"?

3. Unwise use of credit

As of the first quarter of 2017, average household debt in America was

$135,924, for a national total of $12.73 *trillion* dollars. The average American household car loan debt stood at $29,058 ($1.17 trillion), average student loan debt was $50,868 ($1.34 trillion), and average credit card debt was $16,425 ($764 billion), up by 11 percent over the last decade.[2]

What kind of credit debt do you have? Do you know what your interest rates are? If you miss a payment here or there, your interest rate can easily go up to over 30 percent, and you may not even know it. How many credit cards do you have? Do you pay them off in full each month? Are you making only the minimum monthly payments? If you are, do you know how much that's actually costing you? Do you know how long it would take you to pay off your balance at that rate? Remember, being able to make monthly payments does *not* mean being able to afford the purchase.

4. Using a home equity line of credit as a piggy bank

Too many Americans take out a home equity line of credit to fund everyday expenses rather than to pay for purchases that increase the value of their home or that appreciate in value.

5. Living paycheck to paycheck

Something needs to change in your household if all the money you make each month goes toward paying bills.

6. Failure to save some money each month

If you don't have a savings account or if the balance isn't steadily growing, something's wrong.

7. Failure to pay off debt as quickly as possible

How long have you been paying off your debts? Have you made significant "optional" purchases without first paying off debt you already have?

8. Keeping money secrets from your spouse

Do you and your spouse talk regularly (screaming doesn't count) about your budget and how well you're keeping within it? Or do you

keep some of your purchases "secret" in order to avoid unpleasant conversations or shouting matches?

9. Failure to bank at least six months of living expenses

Do you have a contingency fund to help you survive unexpected
emergencies? If your car were to die today, or you found out that ter-
mites had put your home in imminent danger of collapse, how would
you survive?

10. Buying too much house or too expensive of a car

Do you really need a 3,500-square-foot house? Could you own a
smaller one, an older one that's still nice, and not take out such a large
loan? Experts say you should not spend more than about 30 percent
of your income on a mortgage payment. Do you really need to buy
a new car on credit? Could you get an older model instead? A car is a
depreciating asset, and it doesn't make good financial sense to spend
what you don't have on an asset that loses value the moment you drive
it off the lot.

Are you making any of the money mistakes outlined above? If so,
what plan do you have in place to correct the problem? If you have no
plan, how can you start making one? Whatever you do, don't wait! If
you don't know what to do, find a trusted friend who handles money
well and ask for some advice. Despite what the old song says, silence
doesn't lead to anywhere golden.

THREE KEYS TO FINANCIAL HEALTH

How many families can boast of never being in debt? Not far into
marriage, and often even before the wedding itself, many couples begin
to feel "the money strap." It's been said that the number one problem
in marital conflict is communication, and number two is finances. But
I have a theory that the average couple cannot communicate because
they're angry about money. In fact, the "money strap" is probably both
number one *and* number two.

Scripture speaks a great deal about money and our use of it, primarily because if we don't control the money that God puts into our hands, it will soon control us. Did you know that Jesus spoke more about money than about heaven? The number one subject of the Lord's parables is possessions. And the apostle Paul, whom God used to give us thirteen epistles, often wrote of money, offerings, sharing with others, generosity, and related topics.

Rather than try to give you a comprehensive Bible lesson on money management, let me suggest a simple way to begin understanding an effective approach to finances. It has just three main points.

1. Everything Belongs to God

The Lord tells us, "Every beast of the forest is Mine, and the cattle on a thousand hills. I know all the birds of the mountains, and the wild beasts of the field are Mine. If I were hungry, I would not tell you; for the world is Mine, and all its fullness" (Psalm 50:10-12).

Everything we have really belongs to God. We're simply stewards, for a time, of His bounty. That's why we need to learn how to manage it well. For this reason, David prayed as he did when he publicly commissioned the people of Israel to help his son, Solomon, build the temple: "O Lord our God, all this abundance that we have we have prepared to build You a house for Your holy name is from Your hand, and is all Your own" (1 Chronicles 29:16).

2. Give to God Out of Your Firstfruits

To help us remember that God owns everything, the Bible instructs us to give to God and to His work a portion of the "firstfruits" of all the material wealth that comes to us. In doing so, we give thanks to God for His provision, and we set ourselves up for a brighter future. As Proverbs 3:9-10 says, "Honor the Lord with your possessions, and with the firstfruits of all your increase; so your barns will be filled with plenty, and your vats will overflow with new wine." It takes financial discipline to give to God from what we earn at the beginning of the month rather than from what's left over at the end. But that very discipline sets us up for success in life.

3. Position Yourself to Be Generous

People struggling to keep their heads above water financially can't make generosity a part of their lifestyle. When you get a handle on your finances, however, you can start looking for ways to bless others with the money God places in your hands—and I know of few things more satisfying to do. Paul wrote, "You will be enriched in every way to be generous in every way, which through us will produce thanksgiving to God. For the ministry of this service is not only supplying the needs of the saints but is also overflowing in many thanksgivings to God" (2 Corinthians 9:11-12 ESV). Wouldn't you like to prime the pump of "overflowing" thanksgiving to God? If so, then discover how you can become a man who revels in generosity. When you begin with that goal in mind, you will build a household founded on biblical wisdom and financial strength.

FINANCIAL PEACE UNIVERSITY

As a pastor, I have come to see that many people in the church really desire to help advance the kingdom of God. Some of them, however, are new to the Christian faith and are heavily in debt. Others have been Christians for some time yet have never learned how to effectively manage their money.

It amazes me that while we usually don't question the need to teach Christians how to share their faith, or the need to train them how to make disciples, not much is said about teaching them how to handle their money. I believe it is important to teach believers about how God wants His children to manage the money He puts into their hands.

Because Christian men need to develop the mindset of a steward rather than an owner, at our church we make available Dave Ramsey's "Financial Peace University," a resource I highly recommend. Every church needs to have a plan to help its people manage God's assets so that the Lord's people can honor the Scriptures. We can't forget that God requires each of us to be found faithful as stewards.

I have felt greatly blessed to see so many young families (and some not-so-young families) enter our financial training classes. At the end of each nine-week session, we give a personal report to the church about how much debt was paid off by the couples in the class, as well as the average for each couple or individual. We then share how much each person saved, and the percentage increase of their giving. The results have been absolutely remarkable!

THE NECESSITY OF RECEIVING

Every Christian must find a balance between receiving money and giving it. In Philippians 4:15, Paul wrote about both. The words he used are terms related to credit and debit; debit refers to giving, while credit refers to receiving. Some men receive but find it difficult to give, while others like to give but find it difficult to receive.

My primary spiritual gift is exhortation, and after that comes the gift of giving. While I have always loved to give, at one time I did not know how to receive.

In 1977 I was pastoring a small, rural church—Lavonia Baptist Church—in Mooresville, North Carolina. One Wednesday night I was privileged to host a missionary to Indonesia by the name of Sara Snell. Unfortunately, her husband, Roy, was unable to join us for the evening. I still remember how powerfully Sara's message of taking the gospel to the nations affected me.

After Sara spoke that night, she made her way back to Charlotte, North Carolina, where she was staying in a furlough home belonging to Chantilly Baptist Church. It just so happened that a few days later I planned to take my family on vacation to my hometown of Wilmington, North Carolina. A businessman in the church asked me if I would be kind enough to drop off a package for Sara at the missionary residence. I was delighted to honor his request and to accommodate this sweet, godly missionary.

After Sara and I greeted one another, she told me that the Lord had spoken into her heart the night she was with us. Could she tell me what she believed He had said? When I told her to go ahead and share the message, she declared, "The Lord told me that you have a difficult time receiving." At the time, I had always thought that whenever I rejected someone's offer of assistance, I did so simply because I expected God

Himself to provide for my need. I had not yet recognized how God might choose to provide through those who had come to love the ministry God had given me.

After I left Charlotte that night, I reflected on Sara's words. I soon recalled the days after my conversion, when Howard Carter, the owner and manager of Sunset Roller Rink in Wilmington, North Carolina, would often tell me how proud he felt of God's call on my life. He would shake my hand and in my palm I would feel some money he was trying to pass on to me, an investment he desired to make in me and Janet in our early years of ministry. On more than one occasion I embarrassed him by letting the money fall to the ground. "Thank you, Mr. Carter," I'd say, "but I will tell you the Lord is the one who provides for our every need."

Mr. Carter and his wife, Isabelle, once came to spend a weekend at Lavonia Baptist Church. By then he had learned that I did not know how to receive. At one point they visited our home, and for days and even weeks after they left, Janet and I kept finding money hidden in various spots around the house. As we would pull toilet paper from the roll, we would find $10 and $20 bills hidden between the tissues. Janet would remove pots and pans from our cabinets before dinner, and she would find money stashed under the lids. She would find money under our canned goods in the cabinets and in the refrigerator. I can't remember all the places Mr. Carter had hidden the cash.

Today, I am so grateful for Mr. Carter, who has been with the Lord for many years. I treated him ill back in my alcohol-inflamed hoodlum days, before our gracious Lord Jesus saved me and changed me forever. And I embarrassed him in my early days as a believer, before God taught me what I needed to know about money. I will be forever indebted to him and will never forget his generosity. I only wish I had learned the principle of receiving before the Lord called him home.

THE JOY OF GIVING

Janet and I have shared untold joy in being able to receive *and* give. One of the major joys of getting our finances in order was that it put us in a place where we could listen to the Lord as He pointed out needs, and then join Him in meeting those needs.

In the past, whenever someone gave me a monetary gift for doing a wedding or funeral, I would return it to them. But now I take the gift and ask the Lord to show me some person, family, missionary, pastor, or pastor's family who could really use it. I then write the giver a note of appreciation, thanking them for their generosity and investment in my life. I remind them what a privilege it is to be their pastor, and then I describe where I invested their generous gift.

In giving, we actually receive from God. When the apostle Paul received an offering from the Philippian church, he told his friends, "You sent aid once and again for my necessities. Not that I seek the gift, but I seek the fruit that abounds to your account" (Philippians 4:16-17). The phrase "the fruit that abounds to your account" speaks of profit or spiritual blessing. In essence Paul was saying, "We present you with an opportunity to give, not so that we might benefit, but in order that you might benefit. It's not us we are thinking about, but you!"

Because giving and spirituality are inseparably linked, Jesus could rightly say, "Where your treasure is, there your heart will be also" (Matthew 6:21). Martin Luther is stated to have said, "I have held many things in my hands, and I have lost them all. But whatever I have placed in God's hands, that I still possess." How glorious it is to be able to persuade God's people, in absolute truth, to give so that they might benefit.

There is nothing quite like giving. One of my favorite verses about giving comes from Jesus and is found in Luke 6:38: "Give, and it will be given to you: good measure, pressed down, shaken together, and running over will be put into your bosom. For with the same measure that you use, it will be measured back to you." Jesus invites us to picture a long, flowing gown into which God pours a bountiful quantity of grain. And He teaches us that God will load it to overflowing!

Jesus also said, "It is more blessed to give than to receive." Interestingly, you'll find that recorded in Acts 20:35 and nowhere else in the Bible. Some theologians have observed that the reason Jesus's statement doesn't appear in the Gospels is probably because He proclaimed it repeatedly. So evidently, on a regular basis, the Son of God told the crowds following Him, "It is more blessed to give than to receive." If that's accurate, then we ought to work hard and long to become givers.

A TRANSCENDENT PURPOSE

If you want to become a generous giver, you need to get your finances in order. And to make that happen, you need a powerful, transcendent purpose to energize your giving. To get turned around in your finances, *something* in your life needs to get elevated above spending. Until the pain of staying in the same spot financially becomes greater than the pain of making changes in the way you handle your finances, there will be no real change.

I believe nothing can better challenge a believing man to transform the way he handles money than to know he can glorify God through his biblical use of it. I know that I want to glorify God with the income He gives me, and that has motivated me to manage our finances carefully.

One of the seven goals Janet and I have in life is to model generosity. We want generosity to be a lifestyle for us, something we do for as long as possible. As a result, we always give a minimum of a ten percent tithe of everything God gives us. We consider ourselves "firstfruits" givers (Proverbs 3:9), so whether the funds involve royalties from a book, an unexpected gift, an honorarium for speaking, or my weekly salary, we never consider giving back to the Lord anything lower than ten percent.

When it comes to giving, you should have a goal. If you cannot give ten percent now, then start at a lower percentage, and make it your goal to increase that percentage as God increases your capacity to give. The early church father Augustine put it this way: "God has been good to me. He has given me more than I need, yet He has shown me others that need it." That is the way Janet and I feel too as God blesses us. And as our income increases, we give more. I agree with author John Piper:

> God increases our yield so that by giving we can prove our
> yield is not our god. God does not prosper a man's business

so he can move from a Ford to a Cadillac. God prospers a business so that 17,000 unreached peoples can be reached with the gospel. He prospers a business so that twelve percent of the world's population can move a step back from the precipice of starvation.[3]

God performs miracles, and we should take the Lord at His word. The Bible encourages us to believe that as we tithe, He will open the windows of heaven and pour out a greater blessing than we can receive.

THE RESULTS OF
FAITHFUL STEWARDSHIP

Janet and I also practice saving a minimum of ten percent of everything we receive.

My encouragement to you is that you set an amount to give, set an amount to save, and then try to have margin so that if God shows you a special need, you can help fulfill it at some level.

One of the great promises of the Bible is found in Philippians 4:19, which says, "My God shall supply all your need according to His riches in glory by Christ Jesus."

The promise is very personal. He is *my* God.

The promise is very positive. He *shall* supply.

The promise is very pointed. All your *need*.

The promise is plentiful. According to *His riches in glory*.

The promise is powerful. It is *in Christ Jesus*—the safest and most secure place any believer can find himself.

Remember too that Philippians 4:19 is not a standalone verse. It comes in the context of someone who has proven faithful with what God already has given. In *that* context, God promises to meet all of a believer's needs. Paul is a great role model for us.

Who do you know that can model the kind of financially stable and generous lifestyle you'd like to enjoy yourself? Have him over for coffee and discuss your situation with him. Be honest—don't hide anything. Ask for his advice, his counsel, his prayers. See if he'd be willing to help you put together a practical plan that could help you to get on a healthier financial path. No doubt he will tell you some of the mistakes he has made, and how you can avoid them. Listen. Learn. And speak the truth, knowing that brighter days really do lie ahead when you make an effort to grow in this key area of life.

A HAPPY TURNAROUND

I will always remember the day a dear friend and staff member made an appointment to see me in my office. With trembling voice and embarrassment written all over his face, he told me that he wanted me to be among the first to hear that he was filing for bankruptcy.

I sat and listened as he told his story. When he finished, I said to him, "Before you file for bankruptcy, I would like you to visit with our financial planner." I then introduced him to a close friend who had worked in banking and had been a successful builder.

After the two men met several times, the financial planner suggested a strategy unlike anything my indebted friend expected. He took bankruptcy off the table and, in its place, created a clear path of reduced spending and being very aggressive in paying off debt. In just a matter of months, my nearly bankrupt friend became financially liberated and found himself in a good place.

You need to know that my friend, his wife, and their children mean a great deal to me. I had the privilege of leading him to the Lord when he was about ten years old. Years later, he married a girl who, in 1973, had attended the same service in which I myself was converted to Christ. I say all this to emphasize how much this couple means to me. I wanted to see them win just as much as I want *you* to win when it comes to money.

Since those tense days of financial uncertainty, my friend has kept his finances in order. He is a faithful tither and a generous giver to missions causes around the world. He serves in a sports ministry that goes into prisons to share the gospel, a ministry that has led hundreds of men to Christ. He has also been able to buy a home and bless his children with gifts.

I tell his story because, not so long ago, he saw no way out of his deep financial hole, except through bankruptcy. He thought he needed a financial miracle, but with someone else's help, he discovered that by applying sound biblical principles to his use of money, he could become a good steward and experience financial freedom. That which he formerly hid from others he now shares freely with anyone who needs to hear.

And there's no reason to believe that you can't do exactly the same thing.

8

My Wife Talks
Enough for Both of Us

Women talk more than men. A *lot* more. That's just a biological fact, which explains why pleas for husbands to speak up more and enter into feelings-centered conversations with their wives tend to fall on deaf ears (and silent mouths).

There are studies that confirm the fact that women talk more than men. For example, a 2013 study by researchers at the University of Maryland School of Medicine stated that while women speak about 20,000 words a day, men speak only about 7,000—meaning that women speak approximately three times as much as men.

The study, published in the *Journal of Neuroscience*, suggested that a woman's higher level of a "language protein" called FOXP2 "may account for disparities in verbosity" between males and females. Researcher Margaret McCarthy declared that her study's "findings raise the possibility that sex differences in brain and behavior are more pervasive and established earlier than previously appreciated."[1]

But for men who want to keep mostly silent at home, one study does not an ironclad excuse make.

A few months after McCarthy's study was published, an article titled "When it comes to conversation, are women really more likely to be bigger talkers than men?" sharply contested the assertion. The article cited a paper that combined the results of seventy-three studies on the language habits of children and found that

111

girls did speak more words than boys, but only by a negligible amount. Even this small difference was apparent only when they talked to a parent, and was not seen when they were chatting with their friends. Perhaps most significantly it was only seen until the age of two-and-a-half, meaning it might simply reflect the different speeds at which boys and girls develop language skills.[2]

Campbell Leaper, a psychologist from the University of California, Santa Cruz, carried out a meta-analysis of similar studies in adults and found that *men* talked more than women, although once again the difference was slight.

What are we to make of these varying results? That's what can happen when we go to research studies for ammunition either to prove our belief or disprove someone else's. Results can change depending on a researcher's methodologies, audience, test subjects, etc.

Yet another study published in July 2014 in *Scientific Reports* suggested that the key factor in whether men or women talk more has to do with context. At work or in larger meetings, men talk more. In smaller, more social and intimate settings, and in large informal groups, women talk more. The lead researcher for this study, Jukka-Pekka Onnela, assistant professor of biostatistics at Harvard School of Public Health (HSPH), said his team

> collected data using electronic devices on interactions in two different settings—students collaborating on a project, and employees socializing during their lunch breaks. In the first setting, women talked significantly more than men, except in groups of seven or more people when men talked more. In the second setting, there was little difference in talkativeness between genders; differences emerged only for large groups, and here women talked more than men.[3]

Onnela concluded, "It is perhaps surprising that context makes such a big difference."[4]

Sorry, guys, but we don't get off the hook for speaking at home simply by claiming, "My wife talks enough for both of us." If you want a healthy, growing, satisfying marriage, you need to take the initiative to talk.

So what's the answer? Better communication skills?

A HOST OF TECHNIQUES

You don't have to look far online, in books, on videos, in magazine articles, or among marriage counselors to find "Ten secrets to better communication" or "Five discussion secrets that saved my marriage" or "Seven ways to improve your conversations at home." The vast majority of these suggestions involve exhortations to listen more carefully and to show respect while your spouse is speaking. So far as I can see, they're all pretty good.

In no particular order, allow me to reproduce here the kinds of tips commonly offered for helping us to improve our communication with our wives. The list is not exhaustive, but it will give you a good idea of the tips that are frequently recommended.

- Avoid saying "You always…" or "You never…"
- Rephrase and repeat back what you hear your spouse say
- Carefully time your more sensitive conversations
- Use "I" statements rather than "you" statements
- Be open and honest
- Don't say everything you think
- Don't expect your spouse to read your mind
- Express gratitude
- Listen and don't interrupt
- Don't bring up the past
- Don't give unsolicited advice or try to "solve" your wife's problem
- Tell your wife specifically what you love about her
- Take a time-out when you get angry, and resume your conversation later

- Acknowledge your spouse's feelings before you explain
  your position
- Watch your tone
- Make sure you express your wants or needs clearly

In my opinion, every one of these suggestions has merit, along with any number of others not cited above (write love notes, remember that your wife isn't your business partner, empathize with your spouse). I suppose I could unpack a bushel full of such wise recommendations and urge you to learn them, remember them, practice them, and apply them. But I don't think I'll do that.

Don't get me wrong—I'm not choosing to take a different approach because I doubt the value of these suggestions. It's just that I know myself, and I know what happens in my own home when Janet and I get a kink in our hose. While the tips listed above are definitely helpful, in the heat of the moment, we tend to forget them. When that happens, it's not suggestions we need so much as something else. An article from *Psychology Today* provided clarity on this for me.

COMMUNICATION OR CONNECTION?

Steven Stosny, a PsyD writing in *Psychology Today*, doubted whether the communication tips he'd seen in various publications and presentations actually helped marriages all that much. He tended to lump most of them into the same category as the many weight-loss tips he saw everywhere in the media. If they were so effective, he asked, then why weren't more people getting better results?[5]

"It's not that communication tips are inherently bad," he wrote. "The better ones are like the better diet tips: eat less, move more; speak respectfully, listen attentively." He called them "unhelpful," however, because he thought

> they seem to be based on the assumption that marriage
> causes brain damage. When couples describe the early
> part of their relationships, they invariably report that they

communicated very well. (Not many newlyweds mouth the great marriage lament: 'We just can't communicate!') The prevalence of communication tips in the media implies that something about marriage degrades the neurons that embed communication skills. Apparently some married people lose the ability to communicate so completely that droves of therapists and self-help books insist that they must learn and constantly rehearse elaborate techniques to understand each other.[6]

Do you detect as much sarcasm here as I do? But I imagine we both get his point.

What Dr. Stosny says next, however, deeply resonates with me. He claims that good communication in marriage results from good *connection* in marriage, and not the other way around. In other words, we don't connect with our spouse more deeply by learning how to communicate more effectively. Rather, we start communicating better with our mate when we get back to connecting with her as we did at the beginning.

Dr. Stosny writes,

> Problems in love relationships do not occur because people are too stupid to figure out common sense methods of communication or too brain-damaged by the experience of marriage to remember how they used to communicate. In fact, it's misleading to say that people in intimate relationships have communication problems at all, though it can feel that way to them in their frustration and sadness. It is more accurate to say that lovers in distressed and unhappy relationships have *connection* problems.[7]

Dr. Stosny insists that better communication in loving relationships "is a function of emotional connection." When a husband and wife feel connected they tend to communicate just fine, but when they feel disconnected their communication suffers, "regardless of their choice of words and communication techniques."[8]

As I think of my own marriage, Stosny's conclusions seem to ring true. When I'm really connecting with Janet, I don't need to remind myself to tell her specifically what I love about her, or to listen carefully to her words, or to pay attention to her nonverbals. Most of that just happens because I delight in her. I can't get enough. I want to get as close to her as I can, and all those practical helps to communication seem to come naturally.

The problem with depending on communication techniques alone, Stosny says, is that their use can often make your mate feel manipulated. He says this is not merely because the most popular ones "are patently unnatural, more suited for a therapist's office than a living room." Rather, according to him, their use almost always involves a hidden agenda. A common goal, he says, "is not merely to understand your partner or make yourself understood by your partner; it's to manipulate him or her into doing what you want."[9]

I wince at his observation because I recognize some truth there. When Janet and I get into a scrap, I don't really want to hear her position clearly or empathize with her feelings. Rather, I want to win. And if the use of good communication techniques can help me to do that, then great!

Stosny insists that couples don't argue and fight because they lack the right communication techniques, but because they don't believe their partner cares about them or has any true interest in how they feel. They sense a disconnect, in other words. Stosny therefore recommends that rather than try to put into play one or more communication techniques, we ask ourselves a few questions instead:

- Do I want to feel emotionally connected with my partner?
- Do I care how she feels right now?
- How curious am I to learn her perspective?
- What do I love and value about my mate?

Sometimes we get so angry with our partner that we'd honestly have to answer the first two questions with a loud "No!" and the last one with an equally loud "Nothing!" In those cases, it's probably best to cool off first before we continue talking with each other. But make sure the cooling-off session doesn't last long. When our Lord tells us, "Husbands, love your wives, just as Christ also loved the church and gave Himself for her" (Ephesians 5:25), He's not making a mere suggestion. That's a command. And if we want to become the men of God we are called to be, then we must heed that command.

Listen one final time to some wisdom from Dr. Stosny:

> Think of times when you felt emotionally connected to your partner. Communication was not a chore that required techniques, strategies, precision timing, or careful word choice. You were *interested* in him or her. You put things awkwardly all the time, but it didn't matter, because you cared. Emotional connection is a mental state that begins with a resolve to show compassion and love. Early in your relationship you *chose* to feel connected…Forget about communication techniques and choose to feel connected right now. If you do, you'll have a reasonable chance of your partner reciprocating. You will then communicate better. More importantly, you will move closer to recreating a love beyond words.[10]

That sounds like excellent advice to me. *Christian* men, however, have available to them advice that comes from a higher authority—God Himself. And because the Holy Spirit indwells us, we have far greater power to move our hearts from disconnected to connected. Let's briefly consider the resources we have as believers.

COMMUNICATING WITH GRACE

I connect with Janet more deeply and readily when I remind myself of several truths about her:

1. No one knows me better than Janet.
2. No one loves me more deeply than Janet.
3. No one tolerates my inconsistencies more than Janet.

4. No one has forgiven me more than Janet, save the Lord Jesus Christ.

5. No one cares for me and desires for me to succeed in the way Janet does.

Recently as I read Jerry Bridges's book *The Disciplines of Grace*, I was reminded that I need to preach the gospel every day to myself. Marriage is a major vehicle for the gospel's remaking of a man's heart from the inside out, and of his life from the ground up, but that change can't happen unless we yield ourselves to God's commands to husbands, including Ephesians 5:25.

Shortly after reading the book, Janet and I spent a day together. After I brought to our bed her favorite beverage, kissing her and telling her how much I love her, I told her to prepare herself for an Ephesians 5:25 day. I was trying to say that instead of living the day selfishly, I intended, by the grace of God, to love her and focus on her.

One thing is for sure: I am in a relationship with the Lord because He initiated it. And in the same way that Jesus gave Himself for me, I am to give myself for my wife. Jesus gave up His glory and power and became a servant, dying to His own interests and looking to our needs and interests instead. What a tremendous message I send to my wife when I allow the grace of God to be so operative and enabling in my life that I spend large chunks of time listening to her, speaking to her, and caring for her!

Tim Keller stated that if God had the gospel of Jesus in mind when He established marriage, then marriage works only to the degree that it appropriates the pattern of God's self-giving love in Christ. I know of nothing that causes me to get angrier with my wife than when I remain concerned primarily with my own needs.

So the question in my heart at this moment is this: Do my words build up my wife, or do they (or the lack of them) tear her down? Jesus is the pattern for husbands and our model of gracious communication. Luke 4:22 says, "All bore witness to Him, and marveled at the gracious words which proceeded out of His mouth." We expect to hear such a report about Jesus, but because He extended His grace to me, I find sufficient grace not only for my salvation, but also to bring new life to my marital communication. God never intended grace to be a commodity to be treasured in a safe, but to be celebrated in our heart and spoken freely as a means of encouraging others.

The context of Ephesians 5:25 also speaks of Spirit-filled surrender in marriage. If I want to converse with my wife on a deeper level, and if I desire to really hear her heart, then I will have to surrender my life to the Holy Spirit of God. Only then will I have the marriage, the relationship, and the communication that I desire. Once this Spirit-filled surrender begins to take hold in my life, I will increasingly become a Spirit-directed person who is willing to sacrifice my own interests for the well-being of my wife.

I must confess, however, that I am often guilty of listening to my wife only so I can respond. James 1:19 teaches, "Let every man be swift to hear, slow to speak." Too often, I am swift to speak and slow to hear. I have asked God to help me to listen more with my heart.

One of my friends, Dr. Fred Lowery, once gave me a challenge. "Whenever your wife begins to speak to you," he said, "lay aside everything else, give her your undivided attention, and listen carefully to hear what she really says. After she finishes, use these words: 'Tell me more.'" God has greatly used that simple technique through the years. My wife has caught on to it, but nonetheless she loves it.

So then, I must continually ask myself: Have I sacrificed by giving up my time to the person I chose as my lifelong soulmate? As I do this, God willing, I believe I will grow steadily closer to the end of self-assertion. Although I will never forget some of the things I have done, I can move on by no longer remaining imprisoned by them. I expect this to happen as I remember God and all His glory. "Humility is the disappearance of self in the vision that God is all,"[11] said Andrew Murray. May that be the reality of where I'm heading—not merely to listen to Janet so that I might respond, but to listen in order to really hear her and to mean it when I say, "Tell me more."

A CHANCE TO START OVER

As I write all this, I am mindful of one of my favorite proverbs: "A soft answer turns away wrath" (Proverbs 15:1). At times I have made promises to Janet that I would arrive home at a certain time so she would know when to have dinner on the table and we could have a special evening together. Each time we make such plans, I can sense her anticipation in our phone calls or our texts. But there have been times when, for one reason or another, I've arrived late, and I've failed to alert her in advance of my delay. She never has to say a word when that happens; her body language communicates vividly, loudly, and very understandably. Often I try to defend myself. But eventually I have to admit I did not keep my word, so the best thing for me to do is to ask for her forgiveness.

Many years ago, when I had been away traveling for an entire week. I could hardly wait for my plane to land so I could get to my parked car and begin my journey home. As I drove, I talked to my wife almost every mile. I told her how much I missed her, how much I loved her, and how I could not wait to embrace her.

Have you ever had good intentions that went south? And plans that did not turn out at all the way you had hoped?

In just a matter of minutes, I pulled into our driveway. I got out of the car and opened the trunk to grab my luggage. Janet, unbeknownst to me, had slipped around to the back of the car to surprise me with a warm embrace from behind. When she touched me, it scared me almost to death. I responded terribly.

"What under heaven where you thinking about?" I raved. "You scared the daylights out of me!" I followed up with many other harsh words. "I almost hit my head on the trunk of the car. You could have given me a heart attack!"

I watched my wife turn and sadly make her way back toward the house. I stood there for a few moments, still angry at her; and then the anger changed direction. I became very angry at myself for not responding as I should have. So now what should I do?

I got back in the car and drove for a few miles. I cooled off, and asked God to forgive me. I picked up the phone and called Janet. When she answered, I heard a pouting type of voice, and rightly so. I spoke to her as though I had not spoken to her at all that day.

"Hello, darling. I sure do love you. How are you doing? I can hardly wait to get home."

Immediately my soft words melted her heart. "I can't wait to see you either," she replied. "Hurry up; I will be waiting on you!"

In just a few moments, I drove back into that same driveway, got out, and walked to the trunk of my car, but this time expecting an embrace. Sure enough, I was not disappointed. We embraced, told each other how much we loved each other, and I even managed a funny statement: "I had this dream that this other guy pulled up who acted like he was me, but he was a jerk. I don't know who he was, but whoever he was, I am glad he's gone."

We both laughed, went into the house, and had a wonderful evening.

Aren't you glad we can get past our past and start over?

IT CAN SAVE YOUR LIFE

The number of men who love to get together in a large group to pray always amazes me. I see it every year at our men's conferences. They willingly, even eagerly, speak up in those settings. I've always felt blessed when I see men get together to pray.

It's also important, however, that we husbands take time to pray with our wives. Through the years, I have tried to practice not only praying *for* my wife, but also praying *with* her. Often she hears me praying prayers of forgiveness for where I have fallen short, asking for God's cleansing, asking Him to help me love her like Christ loved the church. Yes, prayer is wonderful with a group of men; but it is especially wonderful when it is done as husband and wife.

The Bible declares, "A three-fold cord is not quickly broken" (Ecclesiastes 4:12). In my household, that means Jesus, Janet, and Johnny.

As you read accounts like this, you may feel tempted to think, *Boy, I sure wish I could be like this man of God.* My recommendation: Don't let Janet hear you say anything like that.

Oh, I really wish my life showed no inconsistencies. I wish I could tell you that I never fall short, but I am afraid that Janet would read those words and write a book to tell the truth. Often I have heard her say to those who hear me speak, "How many of you would like to know the real story?" That always causes me to cringe—and remember, *no one* cares for me and desires for me to succeed like Janet does.

My wife's spiritual gift is prophecy—cutting to the chase, seeing through the fog, and getting to the truth. I know she will speak truth to me because she desires for me to live the truth. She wants to help me to become what I claim I desire to be.

Throughout this chapter, I have attempted to be as honest and transparent as I possibly can with the crucial but often very difficult subject of communication. Most of us men constantly work at it, but never perfect it.

At one point a few years ago, I needed to speak to Janet about a growing problem, even though I was not sure how I felt or why I felt as I did. I sensed something that seemed deeper than I could touch and darker than I could shed light on. I'll go into more detail about this in chapter 10, but for now I'll just say I went through a very difficult period. I held my thoughts inside me for a long time and communicated with no one about them, until one morning when Janet said to me, "So, husband, tell me how you *really* feel."

That morning I felt the liberty to tell her, "Honey, I feel like something inside me died."

As I said earlier, Janet typically cuts to the chase, sees through the unreal, questions the sincerity of a peculiar statement, and more times than not, hits a bull's-eye. That morning, instead of having a word for me, my words frightened her. Within minutes she got on the phone with a respected counselor who decided to fly the next day to our sabbatical "home." We spent the entire day in a park, walking and discussing how I felt and how that feeling had brought shame, fear, and guilt into my life.

Had I been unwilling to communicate with my wife, all sorts of terrible things might well have happened. After I began to communicate, not just with my doctor, counselor, and wife, but later with our entire church family and with many friends, I discovered that telling my story opened a door to a flood of people reaching out for help.

I have never been able to fake it in my Christian walk. If I am full of joy, it shows. If I feel sad, it shows. But this time, being honest about what was going on inside me became a lifesaver.

I cannot say enough about the necessity of communication. A key part of that is becoming a better listener. I want to be a man who takes the time required to help others who need to hear from me. I can only hope that all of us men, reticent to speak though we are, will begin to listen and speak in ways that build up others.

9

DUMP THE POISON

M atriarchs and patriarchs have a unique drawing power.
For many years, my wife's grandmother used to host every
Thanksgiving at her house. She was the matriarch, the one who drew
the whole family together. After her passing, it became almost impossible to get all the Allens together again.

Likewise, the Hunts *always* gathered at my mother's house for
Thanksgiving. She was the matriarch of our family. You didn't call her
and say, "We're not coming this year." You just went. But since Ms. Bes-
sie left us, it's hard to gather the Hunts. We all said about Mom, "She's
the glue that holds our family together."

Once the glue's in heaven, however, who takes responsibility to supply new glue?

I've always seen myself as the man of God in our household, long
before some boys came and took my girls away. I forgave them once
they gave me grandbabies. But now that I'm Grandpa, I realize that *I*
have become the patriarch of our family.

I see myself as a sort of protection over my extended family. More
than anything, I want to honor Jesus through my life. I don't want to
bring disgrace to Him or reproach to His name. If I don't live the way I
ought to, my bad behavior could punch some major holes in our family's protective covering. My poor choices could seriously injure my
loved ones. And I know that one of the worst choices I could make,
both for my family and for myself, is to allow bitterness to creep into
my life and so defile everyone I love.

A LONG-LIVED RESENTMENT

Men don't talk much about the bitterness in their souls, but that doesn't mean they never get bitter. Unresolved bitterness has led to some of history's worst male catfights. I can think of several just off the top of my head:

- The Hatfields and the McCoys
- Alexander Hamilton vs. Aaron Burr
- Orson Welles vs. William Randolph Hearst
- Vin Diesel vs. Dwayne "The Rock" Johnson

Do you know what drove every one of those famous feuds? Bitterness. A man said something upsetting, did something unkind, or arranged something cruel that hurt or offended another man. A grudge was born, and eventually one or both men came to see the other as pure evil. Things exploded from there: Vicious insults. Nasty rumors. Fists flying. Lawsuits. Even murder.

I wish I could say that patriarchs are somehow immune to bitterness, but I can't. Not in Bible days, and not today.

I thank God I don't have many regrets about my choices in life, and none of the ones I do have keep me awake at night. I'm grateful I'm neither a Hatfield nor a McCoy. But the regrets I have almost all relate to relationships, and many of them stem from unaddressed bitterness. One of the saddest of them all immediately comes to mind.

N.W. Pridgen was a wonderful man—it was he who first invited me to go to church. Because of him, I'm a Christian today. When he died, his widow called to see if I would participate in his funeral. I told her I would feel deeply honored to do so…until I heard she had already asked someone else to lead the service. She wanted me to play only a supporting role. Even then, I would have agreed to help. But as soon as she named the man she had chosen to officiate, I thought, *Not that guy!* I had held a grudge against this man for years.

It had all started not long after I left the church and town where I had grown to know and love the Pridgen family. This man wanted to taint my testimony. He would say, "You think Johnny Hunt is so wonderful? Did you know this about him?" And he would say negative things about my character and my life. He thought that by pushing me down, he would make himself good.

He started a string of lies, adding new ones every week. People would call me and say, "I just left so-and-so's office. Do you know what he said about you?"

"No," I'd say, "and I don't want to know."

But then I began to get calls from North Carolina, where I was scheduled to speak at a number of churches. Every day, people were calling our church to say, "Pastor Johnny Hunt is coming to our city to speak, but we need to cancel him." The cancellations kept coming, day after day.

Because people were being told lies about me, you can imagine how I felt. The mere mention of this individual's name, coupled with the idea that I'd have to help him lead the service, turned my stomach. Bitterness from the past rose up within me and I quickly built my case for turning down the invitation. Eventually I told the family, "I'm so sorry, but now that I have looked more carefully at my calendar, I realize I won't be able to be there that day." I justified myself—and can be pretty good at that.

Please don't misunderstand. I loved my friend, and I love Jesus above all else. But on that day, I let bitterness rob me of my love for both of them. Bitterness will do that to you. It will redefine what you most value.

Ultimately, we can't be bitter toward someone and still love Jesus as we ought. That means we must let go of our bitterness so we can be all that Jesus wants us to be.

BITTER PATRIARCHS

A patriarch can grow bitter just as easily as any other man. No doubt the most famous patriarchs in the Bible are Abraham, Isaac, and Jacob. Their three names appear together throughout the Scriptures.

But have you ever thought about Abraham, Isaac, and *Esau*?

Jacob and Esau, you may remember, were brothers, the sons of Isaac. Jacob, whose name means "usurper" or "deceiver," lived down to his name for much of his life. He conned his older brother out of his birthright, and later defrauded him out of the coveted patriarchal blessing. When Esau realized that his little brother had gotten the patriarchal blessing, he lost it. Scripture says he "cried with an exceedingly great and bitter cry and said to his father, 'Bless me—me also, O my father!'" (Genesis 27:34). Esau wept aloud, pleading for a blessing as well, but Isaac had nothing more to give. As a result, the Bible says, "Esau hated Jacob because of the blessing with which his father blessed him, and Esau said in his heart, 'The days of mourning for my father are at hand; then I will kill my brother Jacob'" (verse 41).

This is what runaway bitterness looks like.

It starts with an injury, an affront that deeply hurts. The cutting act angers the wounded person because he didn't deserve it. When we're the man wounded, usually we think, *It's not fair!* And we're right; it's not fair. But who said life on a fallen planet would always be fair? Was it "fair" that Jesus got nailed to a cross?

If we don't deal decisively with our feelings about a painful event right away, often our anger "goes underground." We might not rant about it every day, but gradually, over time, it morphs into bitterness. And at some point later—it could be thirty *years* later—when some unfortunate person does something that even *remotely* reminds us of what happened so long ago, we explode. We yell, we scream, we threaten, the veins in our necks bulge out, we want to get back at the other person. Sometimes we rehearse in gory detail every little thing that happened so long before, with such frightening specificity, that the shaken new offender imagines it took place just yesterday. But no, we bellow that it happened *exactly* thirty-three years, five months, four days, and two-and-a-half hours ago. And yes, we *were* counting.

It's not pretty, is it? The fact that we don't talk about bitterness doesn't mean it isn't killing us.

Take a ruthlessly honest look at your own life. Do you harbor feelings of bitterness against anyone? When a certain person's name comes up, does your blood start to boil? When *that* guy walks into the room, do you immediately sprint in the other direction? Do you ever fantasize about a meteor streaking through the sky and vaporizing that guy's car, with him still in it? Or do you secretly plot nasty plans in your mind for how you could get back at him (of course, you tell yourself you'd never actually do anything like that)?

In Jacob and Esau's case, bitterness did not end up in murder, as Esau had fantasized. But it did cause a serious breach between brothers—one that ate at both of them for decades. Esau didn't kill Jacob, even when he had the chance. But Scripture gives us no indication that their relationship ever grew beyond stiff cordiality.

Centuries later, after God freed the Israelites (the descendants of Jacob) from slavery in Egypt, the liberated nation marched for three days into the desert, and then stopped at a watering hole. Unfortunately the water was so bitter that the people couldn't drink it. They became an unruly mob, and started cursing and grumbling and giving up hope that they would survive. The bitter water reflected their own bitter hearts. Moses gave the place a name: *Marah*, which means "bitter."

I find it fascinating that during that entire tense episode, the Israelites were only five miles from Elim, a large oasis boasting twelve springs of water and seventy palm trees (Exodus 15:27). Just five miles! Have you ever considered that in your bitterness, if you would just obey God and trust Him, that maybe you could move from a place of bitterness to an oasis? How far away might you be from an oasis right now?

THE POISON OF BITTERNESS

About twenty years ago a friend shared with me the all-too-true statement, "Bitterness is like drinking poison and waiting for the other person to die." That's not just a contemporary observation; the Bible made the very same connection long ago. In Deuteronomy 32, the Lord contrasts what He expects of His people with how the pagan Canaanites lived. God said of the nations He was about to drive out of the Promised Land, "Their grapes are filled with poison, and their clusters with bitterness" (verse 32 NIV). Bitterness poisons your system.

It creates a smoldering resentment that eventually will burn you up. Many men silently build a life of bitterness from storing up unresolved anger and resentment.

When we fail to cleanse ourselves of the bitterness growing in our hearts, we end up wanting vengeance. We want our pound of flesh. If we don't get an apology, then we want to see some significant hurt inflicted on the one who hurt us. It's only fair, right?

I don't deny that's the way we fallen humans are inclined to think. Left to ourselves, we all go there. I know I do. But the apostle Paul would challenge to us: "You are still of the flesh. For while there is jealousy and strife among you, are you not of the flesh and behaving only in a human way?" (1 Corinthians 3:3 ESV). Every Christian man has the Holy Spirit of God living within him, which means that behaving "only in a human way" denies what Christ has done in our lives. When we act out our bitterness, we call God a liar, who said we *should not* live "only in a human way."

Romans 12:19 declares, "Beloved, do not avenge yourselves." Too often, that's exactly what we would like to do. Wouldn't you agree that sometimes we feel as though God doesn't repay others as fast as we think he should? So we act in His place. Paul continues, "Rather give place to wrath; for it is written, 'Vengeance is Mine, I will repay,' says the Lord."

Note that God says, "Vengeance is *Mine*." When we choose to turn over to Jesus everything that hurts us, we get victory. But what happens when we say, "Vengeance is mine"? Then we move from victory to viciousness. And too often we start talking like this: "Hey, so sorry to hear about his death. When are they doing the funeral? Okay. Yeah, I don't see why I won't be able to come. Uh…could you say that again? You want me to do just the small part, and *he's* going to do the main funeral service? Yes, I see. Uh-huh. But hey, now that I've looked more closely at my schedule…I tell you what—let me get back to you on that."

Paul continues in verse 20, "If your enemy is hungry…"

Absolutely, that's my enemy! So that's exactly how I'll treat him.

"…feed him."

He will starve to death before I take him anything!

"If he is thirsty, give him a drink."

That'll be a cold day in you-know-where before I do that.

When I was an offense to God, the Lord poured mercy and grace upon me. God loved me when I was unlovable. God forgave me when I didn't deserve forgiveness. Nothing in me merited the good things He has done for me, in me, with me, and through me.

Ephesians 4:26 opens with the words, "Be angry." Isn't that amazing? God is giving us permission to be angry! When someone hurts you unjustly, God doesn't expect you to stuff your anger. The problem for us is that the kind of anger Ephesians 4:26 is talking about is *righteous* anger. We know that because the text says, "Be angry *and do not sin*." How can you get angry and not sin? Righteous anger legitimately gets upset over the things that anger God. But we cannot let that anger lead us to wrong thoughts, words, or actions. We cannot allow bitterness to take root in our hearts, or seek vengeance.

Ephesians 4:26 concludes, "Do not let the sun go down on your wrath." If we allow anger to fester, eventually it will boil and turn into wrath. And wrath, left to itself, almost always leads to bitterness.

CUT THE ROOT

One classic New Testament passage on bitterness is Hebrews 12:14-15, which says,

> Pursue peace with all people, and holiness, without which no one will see the Lord: looking carefully lest anyone fall short of the grace of God; lest any root of bitterness springing up cause trouble, and by this many become defiled.

Roots go down, while fruit comes up. Whenever someone hurts you or commits an offense against you, if you don't respond properly, you give opportunity for the "root of bitterness" to grow further down into the soil of your soul.

I'm not much of a gardener, but I know that when I pull weeds from my yard, I have to pull carefully at the base of the weed so that I can yank up the whole plant, including the root. Sometimes I grab a weed, pull, and nothing happens. Its deep roots hold it fast. If I get careless and break off the weed at the surface, then the roots are still left in the ground. When that happens, guess what? In no time at all, the whole noxious weed will grow back again.

The writer of Hebrews says that this "root of bitterness" eventually comes "springing up." *Surprise!* What do we sometimes say when anger comes pouring out of our mouths? We ask, "Where did *that* come from?" And we think, *I thought I'd already dealt with that.* But because we hadn't, it came springing up. For a long time, we didn't see the bitterness. It kept a low profile. But it was lingering just beneath the surface, growing. And then one day, some incident causes it to spring up.

What happens then? As Hebrews 12:15 says, this will "cause trouble, and by this many become defiled." The Greek word translated "defile" refers to dye. It's the word for *stain*, a corruptive influence. If I become a negative, bitter person, even without knowing it, I will spew bitterness on others.

I've been at this place of "springing up," and thank God, others have corrected me. A man once told me that after spending an afternoon with me, he felt like he needed a bath. I had spewed on him without even knowing it. My corruptive words had sprung out of bitterness.

I'm glad every time a brother in Christ writes me a note to say I've been a special encouragement to him and that he wants to follow Jesus more because of spending some time with me. So when I realize I've "defiled" others by pouring out bitterness on them, I cringe.

Before I became a Christian, I cussed and had no idea I was cussing. When I worked as manager of the pool room, if a lady walked in looking for her husband (or if my mom came to find out why I wasn't in school), I had to holler, "Red board! Red board!" That meant we had a lady in the house. I often said other things too.

A guy once said to me, "Johnny, don't talk like that in front of my wife."

Talk like what? I'd been cursing and didn't even know it.

Bitterness, when it takes root, can become like part of your DNA. You can develop a rotten attitude and not even know it. God expects us to be holy—separated from sin and set apart for God—and unless we cooperate with Him in that pursuit, Hebrews 12:14 promises us that we will never even *see* the Lord. Holiness is not an "extra," or merely optional. And you cannot be holy if you harbor bitterness in your heart.

God not only gives us truth, He gives us the power and the ability to obey that truth as we submit to His Spirit. All we have to do is submit. Knowing and believing are just one side of the coin; the other is living and obeying, by His Spirit. For most of us, living and obeying are far harder than knowing and believing! It's not that we don't know what we ought to do. It's not that we don't believe. Rather, it's that we're not willing to live it and obey it. We want to hold on to our bitterness rather than pulling it up by the roots.

Too often we have an intellectual grasp of the doctrines and teachings of Scripture, but we know little of practical Christian living. We've become a generation that can quote the the Bible, define its words in their original languages, but know next to nothing about how to practically live them out.

According to Hebrews 12:14-15, not only is bitterness absolutely opposed to holiness, but its presence causes some of us to "fall short of the grace of God." We fall short not because we can't access God's grace, but because we refuse to appropriate it. Tolerating bitterness in our lives not only guarantees that we will fall short of grace, but that we will "defile" those around us. The language here appears to be borrowed from Deuteronomy 29:18, which warned the Israelites against practicing the horrific sins of the Canaanites: "Make sure there is no root among you that produces such bitter poison" (NIV).

What sort of bitter poison? Let's take a look.

THE BS OF BITTERNESS

Bitterness produces many deadly varieties of poison. Let's consider just a few of them.

Builds Its Case

Bitterness builds its case against those who hurt us. I know this because I have done it myself. It usually starts with a thought like this:

I wouldn't feel this way about him if he hadn't done what he did to me.
We then paint a mental picture of the offender that makes him to be
a monster. Dr. Dick Tibbits, the author of *Forgive to Live*, calls this a
"grievance story." We tell this grievance story to ourselves over and over
again, driving the poisonous root ever deeper into our soul.

Blinds to Future Possibilities

Have you ever known a couple who got married, perhaps even
after dating for a year, but just a few weeks after the wedding the marital wheels started coming off? Sometimes I say to such couples, "Did
you not see this in each other before you got married?" But as the saying goes, love is blind. They didn't *want* to see it. They just wanted to
get married, and so chose not to see anything that might suggest they
should refrain from marrying.

If we are going to hear what God wants to speak to us, then we must
open ourselves up to see what we might not want to see, whether in
ourselves or in others. Bitterness blinds us to future possibilities.

Blocks Spiritual Growth

When you allow bitterness to remain in your heart, its poison blocks
your spiritual growth. If you feel inclined to say, "I'm bitter, but it hasn't
affected me at all," then know that it's already done a number on you.

Blurs Your Vision

A leadership proverb says, "If you don't see it before they see it,
you'll never see it." In other words, leaders need to be able to see far-
ther than their followers. They need to be able to survey a situation and
grasp the big picture—but they can't do this if bitterness has blurred
their vision. Fortunately, God has a remedy for blurred vision: Godly
men with vision clearer than ours who will tell us the truth.

If I sense bitterness in my heart, I know the men I need to talk
to (and not to talk to). These men will give me frank, biblical, hon-
est-before-God advice, and they don't care too much how I respond.
They'll tell me the truth when others won't.

I went into an accountability group one day after being at odds with my best friend. One of the men in my group said, "I'll tell you what, Pastor Johnny. By next Friday, when we meet, let us know your plan of action for bringing corrective measures to your relationship." He paused, then asked this question: "Who could possibly want you and your best friend to not get along?" It certainly wasn't God!

Binds Your Joy

By nature, I'm an optimistic, happy, loving, easygoing person. I'm an "upper" kind of dude. But bitterness can change all that.

When you allow bitterness to reside in you, it will bind your joy. It will leech away your joyous spirit and drain it into Satan's swamp.

Buries Your Peace

Isn't it wonderful to get up in the morning, open your Bible, and have a conscience clear before God and a heart full of peace? Bitterness buries that peace in the graveyard of resentment. If you want to know peace again, you'll need to deal with your bitterness.

Bullies into Bad Behavior

A bitter man is no longer in control of himself; his bitterness takes over. Bitterness will bully you and control both your attitudes and your actions, leading you to take a turn for the worse. When we yield control of ourselves to Jesus, people will want to be around us. But when bitterness takes over, those same people will avoid us.

Blights Your Feelings

Bitterness makes you feel differently about the offender. And when you feel differently, you will act differently. You will stop acting the way you want to act. More specifically, because you are acting on your feelings and not the truth, you will behave like someone who doesn't know God.

"But you don't know what that person did to me," someone will say. "You don't know the pain he caused!"

No, I don't. But are you guiding your life based on God's truth or on your feelings? The Bible says, "You shall know the truth, and the truth shall make you free" (John 8:32). Your feelings, to the contrary, will often keep you in prison.

Blasts Your Hope

The problem with bitterness is that it blasts away your hope. You can't imagine your life getting any better. It has been said that man can live forty days without food, four days without water, four minutes without air, but not one second without hope. The point is this: When you lose hope, you're dead. And bitterness destroys hope.

Betrays Love

Bitterness betrays love. We ought to love all people, but we don't. Bitterness causes us to struggle with some of them. Bitterness slaps us all with the name *Judas*.

FIGHTING BITTERNESS

So what can you do to fight bitterness? I could suggest a bunch of techniques, but ultimately, God wants to show us that our only hope is Jesus.

Frankly, I'm tired of fighting poison with poison. I'd rather fight with the compassion of Christ. And how does His compassion fight bitterness? First, it turns poison into pity. We ask God to help us view the monsters in our lives as flesh-and-blood people in need of grace. The Bible says that Jesus Christ pitied us. What if Jesus had set Himself against me back when I was cursing Him? He chose not to. Instead, He pitied me in my sin. He showed me mercy, kindness, and love—and He's asked me to forgive others as He has forgiven me, for His sake. You don't forgive people for their own sake; you do it for Christ's sake.

Second, you fight bitterness with the grace of God. The Lord's grace is what makes positive changes possible in us. The grace of Jesus does lifesaving surgery on desperately wounded hearts—like mine.

And finally, you admit the truth, *out loud*, and then you do something about it. My favorite New Testament book reminds me, "If you have bitter envy and self-seeking in your hearts, do not boast and lie against the truth" (James 3:14). Don't deny it. Don't keep it a secret. When you speak honestly about your bitterness with a trusted friend, you bring it into the light, and that's a good thing. God Himself tells us, "You were once darkness, but now you are light in the Lord. Walk as children of light" (Ephesians 5:8).

GET YOURSELF FREE

Whenever I ask people to share prayer requests at church, a few hands usually go up. But what happens when I ask for unspoken requests? Hands shoot up all over the place. Why is that?

Some things not only trouble us, but we feel deeply embarrassed even to mention them. We doubt whether anyone else could possibly struggle with the same issue that causes us so much pain. We don't speak up because we don't want others to know our problems and would rather they just pray for us as we pretend to march toward victory.

Think for a moment about the nature of the unspoken requests *you've* made. I'm guessing that a majority of them are relational. If we dared to voice them, we would say things like, "Pray for me. Right now I am just as angry as I can be with _____."

It still hurts every time I think of my refusal to serve at the funeral for my friend. So one day I called my friend's widow and said to her, "I need to talk to you. You'll remember that I didn't come to the funeral."

I'll never forget her reply. She paused, and then said, "You know, my boys didn't understand."

How *could* they have understood? My actions made no sense. Unresolved bitterness never makes sense. I'd done something sinful that I couldn't undo—and bitterness will do the same thing to you. It'll tie you up in knots.

"I really want you to forgive me," I said. Thank God, she did.

The Bible says that in heaven we will know even as we're known. So when I get to heaven, one of the first things I'll say when I see my friend is, "I should've been there."

I believe he will say, "I know. We all have regrets. But Jesus took care of them all!" That hope truly frees me up.

I urge you to admit any bitterness that is in your heart. Then do whatever you need to do to get rid of it. That will free you up—and it will restore within you the hope, joy, and peace God wants you to experience.

10

THERE'S HOPE
FOR DEPRESSION

How would you respond if you received a letter like the following?

> Pastor, please pray for me. I know that I'm saved, but I need to know if saved people go to heaven if they commit suicide.

You'd need to answer such a letter very carefully, wouldn't you? If you simply replied by saying that nothing can separate a believer from the love of Christ, it could almost be like saying, "Hey, why not go to heaven right now?" Your answer could push the individual toward suicide.

I did receive such a letter, and it said a lot more:

> I'm trying to hold on to hear your message this Sunday about depression/suicide, but I really need this question answered. I found myself in this state over the past few months, and the feelings are indescribable. I feel empty, so alone.
>
> I feel like parts of me have died. My brain feels like it's being rewired, and the only message that continues resurfacing is, "Pull the trigger" or "Run your car off the bridge." It's very scary. I'm now waking myself up during the night. I go to work, and I can't concentrate on anything. My head feels

like it's going to explode, and I feel trapped. The thoughts are consuming every aspect of my life, yet I'm forced to go throughout my day making everyone think I'm okay. Right now, the only thing that's kept me from doing this is my children. But when I wake up each day, the first and only thought that enters my head is, *Will today be the day that I go ahead and end it?*

I spent a long time on the phone with this struggling soul. I thank God that we were able to get this person some help. Depression is a serious matter, even among Christians. We cannot just glibly say, "Brother, you're too blessed to be stressed."

MY OWN JOURNEY
INTO DEPRESSION

I know something about depression because I went through a very dark time in my own life. Do you call it hitting bottom? Hitting the wall? I don't know; what I do know is that it meant several months of personal darkness.

It all started one morning when I said something that scared my wife. I remember waking up and telling her that something inside of me had died. Several months of serious depression followed.

More than once during that time I'd written up my resignation as pastor. I felt certain that I did not have the wherewithal to continue to fulfill my ministry responsibilities. During my depression I looked at all my retirement options and tried to figure out what it would cost me in penalties to retire early. I was so downcast I didn't see how I could go on.

Normally I'm a pretty "up" guy. I have a lot of energy and stay on the go, but my bout with depression knocked me off my feet. After I went public about it, other pastors emailed me from around the world. "I can't believe you stood before your large congregation and went on the worldwide web to talk about going through such a difficult time," they told me. And then many of them would add, "Nobody knows about my depression except for the doctor who prescribes my medication." Most of these guys never speak about their problem to anyone, and so they stay alone, in the dark—exactly where depression wants to keep them.

WHAT IS DEPRESSION?

Depression wants to isolate you, to the point you talk to no *one but* yourself. It wants to put you in a dark place, alone, where you can see nothing and feel nothing. It wants to keep you away from your friends and the people who can encourage you.

The highly respected psychiatrist Dr. Keith Ablow has written, "I know depression is every bit as painful as cancer (which studies have proven) and every bit as stealthy."[1] I've had cancer and didn't know it until doctors found it. Sometimes men suffer from depression and no one knows it. That's why we are so shocked when a man seemingly inexplicably attempts or commits suicide.

Those who have never suffered from depression don't realize just how powerfully debilitating it is. Depression causes you to doubt that life will ever return to normal. While many new and wonderful experiences await you in the future, you are unable to see how the darkness could ever end.

Depression wants to drain all hope from you. It wants you to believe you have no chance to move beyond your current dark circumstances. It makes you fear that you'll never feel good again.

Depression distorts your ability to think clearly. That's why you need friends around you who love you, who can speak reason into your heart. Depression causes you to doubt everything—it causes you to doubt yourself, doubt your loved ones and friends, and even doubt God. Depression causes you to doubt love, doubt friendship, doubt God.

Depression will take you to the point you doubt anything good will ever happen again. Rather, all of life becomes a dead-end.

One person from my church wrote, "I've felt the dark cloud and have lived six years with cloudy skies. My doctor increased my medicine for anxiety and depression, but sometimes I still find myself truly jealous of people who have died. Isn't that horrible to say? God has blessed me. I have an awesome family. I have the job that I want. But sometimes, even though I know God is in control and I know all the right verses to read, the depression doesn't go away for very long."

Depression impacts every aspect of a man's life. It affected me spiritually, emotionally, mentally, and relationally—so much that I didn't want to be around people. It affected me physically, giving me feelings of worthlessness, hopelessness, and inappropriate guilt. Because you see no normalcy in your life, you begin to wonder if it's even worth sticking around.

No man is immune to the pain of depression. Every man has felt overwhelmed at some point in his life. *Everyone* has times of feeling sad or depressed.

One of the more astounding things about depression is that, almost without exception, right before the depression hits, the person who becomes victim to it has just experienced some of the highest points in his life. When depression crushed me, I had just surrendered the reins of the largest evangelical Christian body in North America. I had served as president of the Southern Baptist Convention, with its 16 million members. As president, you're the spokesman, asked to speak into just about every issue that arises. During my time in office, I tried to change some denominational policies. The presidency changed me in many ways, and by the end of my term, I was…finished. That's the bottom line. I was done, and I needed some relief.

Many of us assume depression is caused by difficult circumstances. But did you know you can be just as depressed in a mansion in California as you can be on skid row in Atlanta?

Jesus spoke about anxiety, about fearing what *might* happen, when He insisted that every day has enough worries of its own (Matthew 6:34). Too often we build bridges to fearful things that never become reality. Have you ever feared an upcoming meeting, as I have? The majority of the time, however, the meeting would go nowhere near as badly as I'd feared. That's one of the worst things about depression: It lies.

THE LIES OF DEPRESSION

The great prophet of God, Elijah, went through a crippling period of depression, even to the point of having suicidal thoughts. First Kings 19:4

tells us that he "went a day's journey into the wilderness, and came and sat down under a broom tree. And he prayed that he might die." He said, "It is enough! Now, LORD, take my life, for I am no better than my fathers!" When Satan wants to make a lie stick in your life, he will mingle it with more truth than lie. You may try to ascertain where you are by focusing on the truth portion of his deception, without even recognizing the lie he embedded in it. And so you get stuck.

Twice in 1 Kings 19, God asked Elijah why he was so despondent. The prophet responded with a mixture of truth and error, but the lie was what really got him. In verse 10 he said, "I have been very zealous for the LORD." That's true. "For the children of Israel have forsaken Your covenant, torn down your altars." Also true. "And killed Your prophets with the sword." True again. "I alone am left." False!

Elijah basically complained, "Nobody cares, Lord. I'm a caring person, but nobody else cares. I'm the only one left who cares about You— and *this* is how You treat me?" In reality, Elijah was not alone at all. But this is what despair and depression does to a man. Before we know it, we find ourselves believing a litany of lies:

You're losing everything.

Your family will never change.

It's never going to get any better.

No one cares for you.

All false. All lies. And somehow we believe them.

Your depressed self will whisper many such lies to you, and you need to stop listening. Jared Wilson wrote a book titled *Gospel Wakefulness*,[2] in which he said you must defy your depressed self. You must stop listening and start talking. You must preach the gospel over yourself. Every morning I go for a long walk and preach the gospel over myself. One friend told me that it's important we do this, even if we have to get long-winded.

I have to remind myself that I'm not alone. Someone cares for me; the cross of Jesus Christ proves it. My future is not dim; the resurrection assures me of that. We have to tell our depression that its days are numbered. And it helps when we have friends around us who will both listen and tell us the truth.

DEPRESSION AS IMPOSTER

Dr. Ablow called depression "the grand imposter—posing as all-powerful."[3] It appears omnipotent, but you can defeat it by refusing to believe the lies it tells you.

As an imposter, depression insists that nobody cares for you, not even God. It diminishes everything you've ever done and makes you believe that your life has counted for nothing. It paints everything in bleak shades of gray, creating a dreary picture with no hope on the horizon. This is why so many men eventually start asking themselves, *Why live another day?*

Every Sunday I look out over my congregation, full of good friends and their families, mindful of the fact that I have officiated at the funerals of their loved ones after a suicide. Sometimes it was a child. Sometimes it was a parent. Sometimes it was a sibling.

Did you know that every sixteen minutes in the United States, someone commits suicide? About 30,000 Americans die every year from suicide.[4] Suicide occurs among Christians at essentially the same rate as non-Christians.[5] In other words, those who have Bibles in their hands, Christ in their hearts, and family at their side are taking their lives at basically the same rate as those who lack such support.

Suicide kills a disproportionate number of young people and the elderly and has become increasingly prevalent among returning military veterans. That last statistic shocked me. More active duty soldiers now die from suicide than from combat. A 2012 Department of Veterans Affairs study found that, on the average, eighteen to twenty-two veterans kill themselves every day.[6] So each day, some twenty or so people who had put their lives on the line to protect you and me, to keep us free, take their own lives. That's more than 7,000 lives a year. And every suicide leaves behind multiple survivors.

And did you know that one of the major causes of suicide is untreated depression?

Warning signs of suicide include prolonged depression, hopelessness, isolation, withdrawal, loss of interest in usual activities, giving away possessions, suicidal thoughts, and fantasies of suicidal attempts.

I recently reread the story of Walter Thomas White, the former CEO of Voice of the Martyrs, a ministry Janet and I have supported for many years. He killed himself at age sixty-five with a toxic mix of drugs. Here was a man who had spent seventeen months in a Cuban prison, one of the worst jails in the world. His death flabbergasted a lot of people. In April 2012, this grandfather and married father of two went down to the warehouse at Voice of the Martyrs and committed suicide. Only later did we learn that he was being accused of molesting a ten-year-old girl. That threat pushed him into a tailspin. He thought that to be accused of such a heinous crime meant that, for him, there could never be another day.

That's the lie of depression.

One of my sweet church friends wrote me a letter about her husband's suicide. She told me that he had lost a job in the past, but at the time of his death, he had very stable employment. In his anxiety and depression, however, he feared that he would get fired. She's convinced that his fear had a lot to do with his suicide.

And it doesn't really matter who you are or what you do. I know of a very wealthy man who went in for professional counseling after depression started closing in on him. Anxiety and depression eventually overwhelmed him and convinced him he was about to lose everything. Eventually his fear drove him to kill himself.

I know of another man who went to counseling after having an affair. God graciously healed his marriage, but anxiety attacked him anyway. "You're going to lose her," it lied. Eventually he came to believe that his wife hadn't really forgiven him, and one day he took his own life.

Depressed men become suicidal when they lose hope. They forget about the resurrection of Jesus Christ, the one thing in the Christian faith that gives more hope than anything else. Jesus died to defeat sin. He conquered both sin and death when He arose from the grave. The gospel truth is that even in the middle of the worst bouts of depression, we're *never* without hope—yet our adversary can be extremely effective in making us feel as though we are.

SATAN THE DESTROYER

The devil doesn't want merely to inconvenience you, or harass you, or injure you. He wants you dead. He wants to kill you. Jesus warned, "The thief does not come except to steal, and to kill, and to destroy. I have come that they may have life, and that they may have it more abundantly" (John 10:10).

Satan promises the good life, but in the end delivers only death. Peter reminded us, "Be sober, be vigilant; because your adversary the devil walks about like a roaring lion, seeking whom he may devour" (1 Peter 5:8). No wonder Jesus once told some wicked men, "You are of your father the devil, and the desires of your father you want to do. He was a murderer from the beginning, and does not stand in the truth, because there is no truth in him. When he speaks a lie, he speaks from his own resources, for he is a liar and the father of it" (John 8:44).

Why should it surprise any of us that depression is one of Satan's favorite (and most effective) tools? It lies and it kills. Through it, the enemy of your soul will tell you that you have no value, that your life doesn't matter, that you can't make a positive difference. You need to counter his lies and tell yourself that *nothing* done in Jesus's name ever gets wasted. You need to hear what the apostle Paul said: "Your labor is not in vain in the Lord" (1 Corinthians 15:58).

COMPONENTS OF THE HUMAN SOUL

The psalmist once described his soul as "downcast" (Psalm 42:5, 11 NIV). Just for the record, you are a soul. You don't possess one; you *are* one. This becomes particularly important in understanding depression.

God has given you a will that enables you to make decisions. Much that your will decides is based on your thoughts and emotions, which then get acted out in your body. All three of those components—body, will, emotions—are wrapped up in you as a living soul.

Depression has many facets and many causes. Part of depression is mental. Part of it is emotional. Part of it is relational. Part of it is physical. And part of it is spiritual. We're spiritual beings, made in the image of God. I'm not sure which component is most active during depression, but I'm not sure we really need to know. Humans are psychosomatic creatures whose material and immaterial parts both affect them. Depression is often the result of an intricate blend of issues involving both body and soul. But in even the most physiological of depressions, the spiritual element is hardly insignificant. In every case of depression, the spiritual aspect of us may play a larger role than we realize.

There's no doubt my bout with depression was spiritual in nature, but I can't say the spiritual component was the only cause. In fact, what makes depression so difficult to figure out is that you often don't know why you feel so depressed. The uncertainty itself causes anxiety.

THE DARK NIGHT OF THE SOUL

A sixteenth-century Spanish monk known as St. John of the Cross coined the term "dark night of the soul." As John Ortberg has observed, this phrase doesn't refer "simply to the experience of suffering. It is suffering in what feels like the silence of God."[7]

He goes on to observe that in the early days of our walk with God, we delight in devotional activities such as reading the Bible, worshipping God, and praying. But then as we grow, God will call us to a deeper relationship with Him. He may "remove the previous consolation of the soul in order to teach it virtue."[8]

In fact, Ortberg says this kind of dark night can be "God-initiated."[9]

John of the Cross wrote, "God's love is not content to leave us in our weakness, and for this reason He takes us into a dark night. He weans us from all of the pleasures by giving us dry times and inward darkness…"[10]

All of this is designed by God to deepen our spiritual life. Though we may not like this darkness, when we find ourselves in it, we need to wait upon God. And keep in mind that it is a temporary tool God can use to bring us closer to Him, to help us grow

I confess that because of the darkness I went through, I'm a better husband. I'm a more compassionate pastor. I'm a better listener. I pray that I never have to go through depression again! But it has made me a better person. Would I be as willing as I am today to call and help people in distress had I not suffered so long in the dark myself?

SOME HELPFUL STEPS

A team of psychologists helped me to put together a few recommendations on how to combat depression. I'm grateful for every person who helped me assemble this list. Let me suggest eight things you can do when you're depressed.

1. Take consolation from God's Word, clinging to the Lord's promises that He will never leave you or forsake you.

Some men, when they get depressed, can't even climb out of bed. Wives have called me to say, "Pray for my husband; he won't even get up to go to work." This kind of depression is both debilitating and paralyzing.

I could get out of bed during my depression, but I also went to bed very early. About 9:00 p.m., as soon as it got dark, I headed to bed *because that was the only peace I knew.* Instead of wanting to stay in bed once I woke up, I would get up at 4:30 a.m. Why? It wasn't the strength of my faith. I just hoped that God would say something to me in His Word that would help me to make it through another day.

I would start reading my Bible as soon as I got up. I could hardly wait to open it. I would then go on a long walk and talk to my soul. I'd tell my soul what Jesus had told me that morning. You may think I'm crazy, but if you had been there, you already would have thought I was crazy. Hold on to the truth of God's love for you, even when you don't feel it (see 1 Peter 5:7; Hebrews 13:5).

2. Respond to the Holy Spirit if He places his finger on any sin in your life, or on any area He desires to change.

Psalm 139:23-24 says, "Search me, O God, and know my heart; try me, and know my anxieties; and see if there is any wicked way in me." And if there is, then do as the psalmist did: Ask Him to "lead [you] in the way everlasting." That must be your prayer and practice too.

3. Set your mind on truth, despite the lying accusations of the enemy.

As we've seen, the devil will tell you that you have no value. Look to the cross of Jesus and remind yourself that you have immense, eternal value.

4. Reach out to others.

This is critically important. Never discount the power available to you through the encouragement, love, and support of others in the body of Christ!

A depressed man sometimes doesn't need to hear another Scripture verse so much as to receive a hug and a listening ear. A caring heart can do wonders. "I don't know what you're feeling," I've told people, "but I love you and I'm here for you. I'll go the distance with you. Hey, call me at midnight."

A man in my congregation does this for me. For the entire thirty years I've been his pastor, he's told me, "Call me anytime." He occasionally sends me emails: "You haven't forgotten, have you? I'm available anytime. It doesn't matter what you've done or anything you'll ever do; I'll always love you."

How good it is to know you have people like that in your life! They don't love you only so long as you do everything right. Some people *claim* they love you, but when you screw up, they see blood in the water and turn into sharks.

Every depressed person needs a caring heart.

At one time during my depression, I isolated myself. I didn't want to see anyone. I talked to my kids, but I wouldn't take the initiative to go and see them. I didn't want anyone near me. It was just Janet and me, and eventually our counselor.

Eventually, however, I got to really missing my friends. One day I called one of them and said, "I'm dying for fellowship. I've been out for a while. I'm in Tennessee. Would you come and meet me? I really, really need a friend." And he came.

A depressed lady once told me that, the night before, she'd slept with a gun beside her. We spoke on the phone for a long time. She later sent me a Facebook post saying, "You'll never know how much your call encouraged me."

A missionary called me and said, "My daughter has been in deep depression for three months. Could you pray for her?" I didn't just pray for her; I asked for her number and called. It just so happened that Janet and I were in her part of the world, so we made an appointment to take her to dinner. We spent a good couple of hours with her, just listening.

5. Pursue counseling to discover and change the unhealthy ways that you may be dealing with life.

When I told Janet that something inside of me had died, the next morning a counselor flew out to meet us. We met in a park. Despite the heat, we spent all day walking in the park, talking, sharing, trying to make sense of life. I had some unhealthy ways in me, some distorted thinking. He listened, had a caring heart, and helped me.

6. Take necessary steps to improve your overall health, such as a diet, exercise, and proper rest.

During the months of my depression, I'd get up at 4:30 a.m. Eventually Janet would come into the room and ask, "How was your walk?"

"I didn't walk this morning," I might say.

She'd immediately return to our bedroom, open a drawer, pull out my running shorts and a shirt, get my tennis shoes, come back to me, and say, "Okay. Get them on, buster. Let's go."

"I'm not going today," I'd say.

"I'm going to stand here until you do," she'd announce. And if you've ever seen the way Janet can look at you…I'd rather just go for a walk. When the pain of staying the same became greater than the pain of change, I went walking.

To this day, I still walk. Every doctor or psychologist I've ever read says that exercise helps a man deal with depression. That's why I'm so aggressive on exercise.

7. Talk to your medical doctor about your depression and possible medical treatment.

I told my doctor how I felt. So long as I live, I'll never forget his reply. "You're getting older," he said, matter-of-factly. In that moment,

I felt like the preacher who voiced his own complaints to his doctor. His doctor said to him, as mine did to me, "Well, you're getting older." The preacher didn't like that answer and replied, "I'll get a second opinion." The doctor said, "I'll give you that too. You're ugly."

My doctor explained to me, "Listen, you're sixty-two years old. You're an older man. Your body has changed."

Medicine can help in some cases, just as a cast can help when you break an arm. I won't say no to either the cast or the medicine. Sometimes a chemical imbalance in your brain needs medical intervention, just as you may need medicine to cure a dangerous infection. If we don't consider it a lack of faith to take antibiotics to kill deadly germs inside our bodies, then why should we consider it a lack of faith to take medicine to help re-establish a healthy chemical balance in our brains? Someone once told me, "Pastor, I heard that if I just had enough faith, I wouldn't take the depression medicine. So I got off the medicine and later that week I tried to kill myself."

James Dobson has greatly influenced me through his writings. I've even had the privilege of being with him several times. He said that when you're really depressed, the first thing you should do is go see your medical doctor. My doctor gave me a prescription and said, "If you get to where you can't sleep—if it gets unbearable—this may help you to rest. It may help you with your anxiety."

Let your doctor be the doctor. Take his advice. If you're having thoughts of suicide, get to the hospital right away. Go straight to the emergency room. Many places have a 1-800 suicide number. Call it. Get someone to talk to.

And always be supportive of someone pursuing professional and medical help. They may need it more than you know.

8. Keep praying and be sure to give thanks.

During my very dark time, I would lay on my face. I followed Adrian Rogers's advice: You can sit and pray when it isn't too bad. When it gets real bad, drop to your knees. When it grows worse, fall on your face. And when it gets even worse than that, dig a hole and lower your nose into it. In that hole, I would get down and say, "God, I'd appreciate it if You'd bring me out. Would You use the body of Christ, use my counselor, use my medical doctor to help me? I don't want to stay here."

When you are depressed, I believe it is important, as much as you can, to give God praise and thanks for His work in your life and in the lives of others. When you pray only about the tough things happening in your life, that's where your mind tends to stay. That's why Paul said, "Do not be anxious about anything, but in every situation, by prayer and petition, *with thanksgiving*, present your requests to God" (Philippians 4:6 NIV; emphasis added).

TALK ABOUT IT

Jesus came to comfort those who mourn. He came to set at liberty those who are oppressed, downtrodden, downcast, depressed, and sorrowful (Luke 4:18).

Isaiah 61:3 promises that the Messiah will exchange beauty for ashes, the oil of joy for mourning, the garment of praise for a spirit of heaviness. Does a heaviness lay over your heart today? If so, I pray that you may soon be called a tree of righteousness so that the Lord may be glorified. Most important of all, don't choose to suffer in silence with your depression. Talk about it. Let others know. Don't shut people out.

I pray that the bright, shining light of God's Word and His Son would give you hope. There *is* hope for depression! As a minister of the gospel of Jesus Christ and one who came out of a very dark place, I want to tell you:

There's hope for depression!

11

IN THE
TORMENTER'S HAND

More relationships have been broken, more marriages ruined, more churches destroyed by a lack of forgiveness than by any other cause. You might assume, therefore, that we'd want to talk about it. How could we refuse to speak about something that inflicts so much damage and pain?

In fact, though, we men generally don't even think about our failure to forgive until our lives become unbearable.

One day after I had preached a sermon on forgiveness, a downcast man came to see me. "I've been captive by my lack of forgiveness for years," he admitted. For him, confessing the ugly truth and getting it out in the open was the first step to getting his life back on course.

Jesus insists that forgiveness must come from the heart. And if you have refused to forgive someone, you need to know that you're in bondage. The Bible even says that Jesus will turn you over to the tormentors.

FORGIVENESS DOESN'T
COME NATURALLY

Forgiveness doesn't come naturally to most of us. Men, by and large, find it difficult to forgive those who have hurt them deeply. King Louis XII spoke for many people when he said, "Nothing smells so sweet as the dead body of your enemy."

Who among us can't name some deep hurt in our lives? Perhaps even right now you are separated from your spouse. Maybe she has already moved in with someone else. You may say, "She needs to get right with God!" You're right; but if you don't handle the situation well, you'll find yourself right along with her, in bondage to sin. Your unwillingness to forgive will lead to a kind of personal torment you can't even imagine. Jesus said you need to forgive others *from your heart.*

It isn't easy.

One day the apostle Peter asked Jesus a crucial question about forgiveness. You should thank God for Peter, because he was always willing to ask what everyone else was thinking.

"Lord," Peter said, "how often shall my brother sin against me, and I forgive him? Up to seven times?" (Matthew 18:21). Rabbinical law taught that when someone had sinned against you, you should forgive him three times. Simon Peter probably wanted to show his generosity, so he thought, *I'll double it and add one for good measure.*

Jesus replied, "I do not say to you, up to seven times, but up to seventy times seven."

Four hundred and ninety times? That's a lot of times to forgive the same person for the same offense! The passage suggests that while we work in the context of addition, Jesus works in the context of multiplication. For all practical purposes, He's saying, "The correct number is beyond counting."

To make sure that Peter and the rest of the disciples got the point, Jesus then told a memorable story about forgiveness and unforgiveness—about the blessings of the former and the consequences of the latter.

> Therefore the kingdom of heaven is like a certain king who wanted to settle accounts with his servants. And when he had begun to settle accounts, one was brought to him who owed him ten thousand talents. But as he was not able to pay, his master commanded that he be sold, with his wife and children and all that he had, and that payment be made. The servant therefore fell down before him, saying, "Master, have patience with me, and I will pay you all."

Then the master of that servant was moved with compassion, released him, and forgave him the debt.

But that servant went out and found one of his fellow servants who owed him a hundred denarii; and he laid hands on him and took him by the throat, saying, "Pay me what you owe!" So his fellow servant fell down at his feet and begged him, saying, "Have patience with me, and I will pay you all." And he would not, but went and threw him into prison till he should pay the debt.

So when his fellow servants saw what had been done, they were very grieved, and came and told their master all that had been done. Then his master, after he had called him, said to him, "You wicked servant! I forgave you all that debt because you begged me. Should you not also have had compassion on your fellow servant, just as I had pity on you?" And his master was angry, and delivered him to the torturers until he should pay all that was due to him.

So My heavenly Father also will do to you if each of you, from his heart, does not forgive his brother his trespasses (verses 23-35).

Unless we understand the gargantuan difference between owing someone 10,000 talents as opposed to 100 denarii, we will never understand the point of Jesus's story. So how much is 10,000 talents?

In the economy of that day, a talent was the largest denomination of currency in the Roman Empire. A man would have to work twenty years to earn just one talent. A governor could support a whole region of Palestine on 800 talents a year. The highest number for which the ancient Greek language had a specific term was 10,000. So 10,000 talents was on the borderline of what the ancient mind could imagine in terms of money. This servant owed more than anyone's mind could fathom, and without question it exceeded anything he could pay back in his lifetime. William Barclay wrote that it would take an army of 8,600 men, each soldier carrying a sack of 60 pounds on his back, to lug all that money.[1] Barclay said that if you put those men in a line and asked them to stand one yard apart, the line would stretch five miles. And yet the king forgave his servant of this mammoth debt simply because the king had pity on the groveling man.

Now compare that enormous debt to the measly 100 denarii owed by the second servant. A man could easily carry 100 denarii in his pocket. An average servant could earn that kind of money in three months.

The difference between the two debts is not just apples and oranges; it's atoms and galaxies. You'd think that the first servant would have been so giddy about the king forgiving his vast debt that he'd gladly reciprocate, maybe even inviting the second servant to a party to celebrate together their canceled debts. But no. Instead, the forgiven servant grabbed the second servant by the throat and demanded immediate payment. When the second man couldn't comply, the first servant had him thrown into debtor's prison.

This kind of malicious behavior seems unthinkable, even bizarre. It's hard to believe a man could act in such a mindless way—and that's exactly the Lord's point to Peter. For a Christian to be unwilling to forgive anyone is unthinkable, even bizarre.

WE ALL OWE MORE
THAN THE FIRST SERVANT

How much did Jesus forgive us at Calvary? We all owe to God a debt that is infinitely greater than 10,000 talents. None of us could ever repay it.

"But I've been a good person," someone may say. "Although I've never trusted Jesus as my Lord and Savior, I've been pretty good. I think God will understand. When He weighs my good deeds beside my bad ones, I think I'll come out okay."

Are you *kidding*? Through this story, Jesus is trying to help us understand that *no one* has any possible way to pay his own debt of sin. *No one* can work his way to God. *No one* can earn his way to heaven. *No one* even remotely deserves to go there. We all owe more to God than any of us could ever pay in our lifetime, or in a thousand lifetimes. We all stand under the righteous judgment of God, for He says the wages of sin is death (Romans 6:23).

But God had mercy on us, He pitied us, and the moment we placed our faith in Jesus Christ, He forgave us the entire debt. He canceled *all* our liability. He removed *all* our sin from us, as far as east is from the west (see Psalm 103:12). He buried it all in the sea of forgetfulness, never to remember it again. We can't even conceive of how much we owed the Lord, and yet He has forgiven us of it all.

How, then, could we ever refuse to forgive anyone who has hurt us? You can't tell me of any comparative situation that even *remotely* equates the debt you owed to God (galaxies) with any debt owed to you (atoms).

Note the word Jesus used to describe the unforgiving servant. The king said to the man, "You *wicked* servant." The Lord Jesus Christ declares that if you're a Christian and yet you refuse to forgive someone who has hurt you, you are just like that wicked servant. When God in His grace forgives you of a debt you couldn't pay, and then somebody wrongs you and yet somehow you think you're justified in refusing to forgive him, you become wicked. *Wicked!*

INTO THE TORMENTOR'S HANDS

The enraged king told the unforgiving servant, "I forgave you all that debt because you begged me" (Matthew 18:32). The king then demanded, "Should you not also have had compassion on your fellow servant, just as I had pity on you?" (verse 33).

The answer, of course, is yes. But the servant had said no. So what happened?

"And his master was angry," Jesus said, "and delivered him to the torturers" (verse 34).

One Sunday after I preached a sermon on unforgiveness, a man approached me and said, "You just ate my lunch with that sermon. I'm in bondage. I have refused to forgive a man who wronged me, and it has been tormenting me." He felt that way not because he had hurt someone, but because someone had hurt *him*, and he had refused to let go of the hurt.

Many of us assume that when another person offends us, it's that person who has the problem, regardless of our response. We imagine that God doesn't even consider our response to be a part of the picture. But Jesus tells us, "Think again."

You may be the innocent bystander. Maybe someone attacked you, criticized you, offended you somehow, and he refuses to make amends. Clearly, he's in the wrong. But if you don't watch yourself, after a while, you'll begin to resent that person. You'll harbor unforgiveness in your heart. And here's the tough part: *You're* the one who gets turned over to the tormentor. *You're* the one in bondage, when God desires for you to be free.

The good news is that you don't have to stay there. Jesus said the king delivered the unforgiving servant to the tormenters "until he should pay all that was due to him" (verse 34). The question is, what did the first servant still owe the king? He didn't owe him the 10,000 talents; the king already had forgiven that debt. So what debt did the man still owe?

The servant still had an ongoing obligation to forgive others, just as he himself had been forgiven. Until he became willing to pay *that* debt, he would stay locked up and subject to the tormentors.

And so will you and I.

A HALLMARK OF ALL BELIEVERS

If Jesus had spoken so solemnly in only this single passage about the importance of forgiveness, then maybe we could try to understand His words in a different way. But in fact, Jesus made this message about forgiveness an important theme of His teaching.

When the disciples asked the Lord to coach them on how to pray, He gave them what we call the Lord's Prayer. And He added, "If you forgive men their trespasses, your heavenly Father will also forgive you. But if you do not forgive men their trespasses, neither will your Father forgive your trespasses" (Matthew 6:14-15).

Jesus went a step further. He said, "Whenever you stand praying, if you have anything against anyone, forgive him, that your Father in heaven may also forgive you your trespasses. But if ye do not forgive, neither will your Father in heaven forgive your trespasses" (Mark 11:25-26). Luke 6:37 gives us yet another echo of this theme: "Judge not, and you shall not be judged. Condemn not, and you shall not be condemned. Forgive, and you will be forgiven." That's what I call a consistent message.

Several years after Jesus's ascension into heaven, His Spirit inspired the apostle Paul to write, "Forgiving one another, if anyone has a complaint against another; even as Christ forgave you, so you also must do" (Colossians 3:13). To another group of Christians Paul wrote, "Be kind to one another, tenderhearted, forgiving one another, even as God in Christ forgave you" (Ephesians 4:32).

When Jesus put forgiveness so highly on His to-do list, He was merely following the pattern of His Father. Psalm 78:38 reminds us that God, "full of compassion, forgave their iniquity, and did not destroy them. Yes, many a time He turned His anger away, and did not stir up all His wrath." In a similar way, the psalmist prays, "For You, LORD, are good, and ready to forgive, and abundant in mercy to all those who call upon You" (Psalm 86:5). From the very beginning, God has called upon *all* His children to mimic His willingness to forgive. He intends it as a hallmark of everyone in His family.

THE RESULTS OF UNFORGIVENESS

When a man refuses to forgive from his heart, there are several unpleasant results, none of them good:

1. It results in ingratitude.

We could write the title "Ungrateful" over the story of Matthew 18. The servant forgiven of a colossal debt should have been one happy camper. He should have been grateful. He should have sung the praises of almighty God. Instead, he displayed mountains of ingratitude.

We know he was ungrateful because the first thing he did after being forgiven was to find a man who owed him a handful of change. He grabbed him by the throat and demanded to be paid. When the second man asked for more time to cover the debt—exactly what the first man had asked of the king—the first man had the second one thrown into prison. How ungrateful!

To be unforgiving is to be ungrateful. To say, "I've been wronged and I believe I'm justified in carrying a grudge" shows clearly that a spirit of ingratitude has overrun your heart.

2. It causes you try to hold someone hostage.

When a person is taken hostage, the abductors usually want something in exchange for his return: money, weapons, the release of prisoners. They state, "If you give us what we want, we will give back the person we've taken." There's always a condition attached, a ransom demand of some sort.

When we refuse to forgive others for the wrongs done to us, we are saying essentially the same thing as the hostage-takers. We try to hold offenders hostage until we get our demands met. We don't ask for money, but instead demand that they makes things right. And until they do, we withhold forgiveness from them.

Suppose someone hurts you, then something bad happens to that person. If you respond, "He's getting exactly what he deserved," you are displaying hard evidence of an unforgiving heart. God wants you to deal with it. The peace of God and the joy of Jesus Christ will never flow through the heart of an unforgiving person.

3. It keeps you from understanding the grace of God.

God helps us to understand His grace not only by forgiving us, but by enabling us to forgive others. Grace makes us increasingly like Jesus, who willingly forgave others.

If there is any one person in the Bible who truly understood the extent of God's grace, at least from an earthly perspective, it would be Joseph. His brothers hated him, envied him, cast him into a pit, and sold him into slavery. Then they went home and told their dad that a wild animal had killed Joseph. After everything Joseph's brothers had done to him, he somehow found the strength to forgive them all.

Not only did Joseph genuinely forgive his brothers from the heart, he even believed that God had allowed them to treat him in such a despicable way in order to bring good out of their evil. He could rejoice in what had happened despite the many years of very deep personal pain it had caused him. What a work of God! If the Lord could do that in Joseph's life, then what could He do through you when you become willing to forgive?

4. It erects a barrier.

Have you ever had a spat with your wife? When that happens, things can get ugly. A barrier might even go up between you two.

But when one of you gets right with God and reaches out to the other, that's the first step to removing the barrier. When you do that, it allows you to restore your relationship.

When two men get crossways with each other, things can get ugly as well. Perhaps they've been good friends. They're brothers in Christ, and they both love Jesus. But then something happens and a barrier goes up. Immediately that wall of unforgiveness cuts off all reservoirs of love, joy, acceptance, and caring. Only when they become willing to say, by an act of the will, "This is crazy! It's being in bondage. It's being turned over to the tormentors. In Jesus's name, I choose to forgive" does something amazing happen. Once that barrier of unforgiveness goes down, all the old, pleasant feelings of friendship will come flowing back. Restoration brings real joy! I believe this because I have experienced it.

5. It delivers you to the tormentors.

The Bible teaches us that forgiveness liberates. It frees us from a heavy load of guilt, bitterness, and long-harbored anger. Unforgiveness, by contrast, cripples your faith. The poison of an unforgiving spirit permeates your entire life, separating you from fellowship with God, your friends, and your family. And unforgiveness can never be legitimately defended. Never!

THE ELEMENTS OF FORGIVENESS

Forgiveness is an act of the will. Charles Stanley wrote a wonderful little book on forgiveness in which he said that forgiveness always involves three elements.

1. Someone injures you.

Somebody hurts you, perhaps through another relationship. However they hurt you, they caused you some injury.

2. A debt results from the injury.

As a result of the injury, a debt is created: "Do you know what that person did to me? He owes me!" Whenever someone injures another, an obligation exists to right the wrong. The offending party has a duty to apologize, to pay back the debt, to set things right.

3. The debt must be cancelled.

One way or another, the debt must be erased. It's easiest when the offending party says, "I was wrong to do that, please forgive me. What can I do to make things right?" But often the offender never admits his wrong, never asks for forgiveness, and never seeks to right the wrong. Does that mean you're stuck?

No, it doesn't. *Regardless of what the offender may do*, Jesus calls believers to forgive the debt, which, in turn, releases that wounded believer from the hands of the tormentor. Bitterness has no grip on the heart of such a believer.

One man said to me, "You don't understand! My wife and I have two beautiful little children. Everything was going fine. I have worked and worked and worked so she could stay at home, only to find out that while I was at work, she was seeing someone else. She ran off with him and left me with the kids. It seems like that's the end. She's ruined my life! I can't go on from here, and I can't forgive her for what she did." I told him, "Yes, you can go on from there, but you have to start by forgiving her from your heart."

No one can truly forgive from the heart, of course, apart from the help of the Holy Spirit of God. That's what is so wonderful about the Christian family! Only Jesus Christ, through His Spirit and His church, can make this process work.

THE REAL LOSER

A man with an unforgiving spirit is always and forever the real loser. If we refuse to deal with our unforgiveness, which inevitably results in bitterness and resentment that puts us in bondage, we cannot have the kind of fellowship with the Father and with the family of God that Jesus died and rose again to give us.

Perhaps years ago someone offended you and you never forgave him—and you know it. Perhaps the Spirit of God is, right this moment, resurrecting in your mind the name of this person. To this day, you have an unforgiving attitude toward him.

You may say, "Johnny, let it go. All you're doing is bringing up old wounds created a long time ago." But if you still feel the kind of pain that makes you say such things, then I can assure you that you've never dealt with the issue as Jesus demands. If you say, "I plan to leave it right where it is, in the past, and I'll go on with my life," then you will never know what a real, genuine, trusting relationship with another brother and sister is.

If you're in the tormentor's hand, know that it will affect *every* relationship you have. That's why many people say, "I find it difficult to trust anyone; I've been deeply hurt in the past." When you honestly deal with that issue at Calvary, you won't have nearly so much trouble trusting people again.

HOW CAN YOU KNOW FOR SURE?

How you can know whether you've *truly* forgiven someone? Suppose you've been hurt by someone and you've refused to forgive him. One day you see him down an aisle at the grocery store. At that moment, you'd rather turn around and duck into another aisle. Why? You don't want to interact with the man because you've never forgiven him from your heart. In your mind you may have forgiven him, but deep in the recesses of your heart, you just can't face him with liberty. Do you know why? You're in bondage.

Imagine that you see five people standing in a circle and having a great time. When you take a closer look, you notice that one person in the group is someone you seriously dislike. Deep in your heart, you harbor a grudge against him.

This leaves you with two options. First, you can avoid the entire group because of your attitude toward the one man. Or second, you can summon up courage, join the group, and interact with four of the people while giving a cold shoulder to the one you dislike. This is your way of saying, "I haven't forgotten, old buddy. I've got your number."

In reality, it's the devil who has *your* number. You're right where Satan wants you.

When you have an unforgiving heart, you refuse to love the person who hurt you. You refuse to accept him or respect him or say a good word about him. You just can't find it in your heart to say anything kind about him—and the whole time, you actually feel good about it. The devil pats you on the back, saying, "Attaboy! You're doing a good job. You've got him right where you want him." But the truth is, again, the devil has *you* right where he wants you.

Jesus said if you refuse to forgive someone, you are in bondage—and you won't get out until you forgive. Forgiveness is the act of setting someone free from an obligation incurred by wronging you.

All of us, at one time or another, have received forgiveness. And yet we all feel tempted to hold grudges, allowing resentment to set in and put up a barrier. Sometimes we realize when we are withholding forgiveness, and other times we honestly don't. So how can you tell when you've fallen into this deadly trap?

An unforgiving attitude sounds like this: "I can't *stand* to be in that man's presence." When you say (or leave unspoken) statements like that, know that you're in the grip of unforgiveness.

Unforgiveness is a bondage that stifles your ability to love and accept others. It's a kind of slavery that chokes out the abundant life that Jesus Christ promises to everyone who will believe. Unforgiveness also makes no sense. If God forgave you for everything wrong you've done in the past, everything wrong you're doing in the present, and everything wrong you will do in the future, then what right do you have to refuse to forgive anyone?

You may say, "Johnny, I've forgiven those who have hurt me." But have you *truly* forgiven them?

FOUR ATTITUDE CHECKS

Let me give you four attitude checks so you can determine whether you've truly forgiven someone who has hurt you.

1. *Your negative feelings start to disappear.*

Do you still feel angry when you see the person or hear his name mentioned? When you've truly forgiven someone, you don't feel the same anger you used to when you unexpectedly run into him.

2. *It's easier to accept the person who hurt you without feeling the need for him to change.*

When you truly forgive someone, even if he *never* changes, you're still free. You no longer feel the compulsion to manipulate him into asking for your forgiveness or telling you how sorry he feels for hurting you. You're free!

3. *You have a new appreciation for that person's situation.*

Maybe you've left a church because of a difficult situation in which you felt unfairly treated. Understand that you'll never be what God wants you to be in your new fellowship until you deal with your unwillingness to forgive someone in your former fellowship. The problem will still exist no matter how far away you move! The anger you felt when you lived across the street from someone will still come up in your mind when you're thousands of miles away. Once the blinders of resentment are removed, however, you can start to understand from the other person's perspective what happened and why. And you will likely discover he isn't the demon you had made him out to be.

4. *Your concern about the needs of the other individual will outweigh your concern about what he did to you.*

As fallen humans, we tend to be selfish and self-centered. We ask,

"Do you know what he did to me? Do you realize how he hurt me?" I recommend that you study the cross in all four Gospels. Remind yourself of what *you* did to Jesus at Calvary. As you reflect on His sacrifice for you, the offense that you have considered to be a "big deal" will begin to fade into oblivion. In its place, you may find growing in your heart a genuine concern for the other person. That, my friend, is a genuine work of the Holy Spirit of God.

And it's a work you and I desperately need.

PART 3:

A Place to Untie Our Tongues

12

You Need More
Male Friends

W hen it comes to speaking up about our struggles, there are some
definite steps we can take. The best part is, God doesn't ask us
to go it alone. He has given us resources that can help us in those
times we're inclined to stay silent. Whether our battle is with pornography, alcohol, depression, or some other difficulty, God stands ready to
help—through the encouragement, wisdom, and friendships of other
men. That's going to be our focus for the rest of this book.

AN EVER-PRESENT DIFFICULTY

Back in 1983, David W. Smith published a compelling book titled
The Friendless American Male. Smith discussed the extreme difficulty
most American men have with trying to create and sustain real, solid
friendships. He talked about the high cost of being male, how men and
women differ in their friend-making habits, and much more.

Thirty-five years later, I don't know that much has changed.

Although the publisher of Smith's book no longer exists, the problem still does, and in spades. Most guys I know tend to call a couple
of acquaintances their "friends" and let it go at that. They try to navigate the complexities of modern life mostly on their own. At church,
they may smile and nod and shake hands with a few others, but if you
were to ask any of those hand-shakers for any significant detail about

his life—when he committed himself to Jesus, for example, or where he grew up—you'd more than likely get blank looks.

Brothers, we just *can't* settle for that. Far too much is at stake.

WHO LIFTS YOU UP?

One of my favorite stories about the importance of friends comes from Exodus 17. Moses was standing high on the mountain while the Israelites fought the Amalekites down in the valley. Moses lifted up the rod of God, the symbol of the Lord's power, asking God for victory. As he prayed, his arms became weary and began to fall. As he lowered the rod of God, the Amalekites prevailed; when he raised up the rod of God, the Israelites prevailed.

As Moses's weariness got worse, God sent two friends, Aaron and Hur, who seated Moses on a rock. The friends then held up his arms, one on each side. As a result, Israel prevailed that day. Exodus 17:12 says that Moses's hands "were steady until the going down of the sun."

That I would have such friends has always been my prayer. One day the sun will set on the lives that God has given us. We will realize then, maybe like never before, how the many people whom God surrounded us with have held up our hands and helped us prevail. None of us have reached where we are on our own. It took friends to get us here.

For good reason Scripture therefore says, "Two are better than one, because they have a good reward for their labor. For if they fall, one will lift up his companion. But woe to him who is alone when he falls, for he has no one to help him up" (Ecclesiastes 4:9-10).

Wherever you look in the Bible, you will see that the men who accomplished great things for God always had companions, helpers, friends who came to their aid. None of them had success on their own. Consider David, who, despite his flaws, is still remembered as the greatest king of Israel. He earned such a revered name that even Jesus Christ Himself is known as "the son of David" (see, for example, Matthew 1:1).

But would David ever have lived through his early adult life without the help of his closest friend, Jonathan? When Jonathan, the eldest son of King Saul, heard how a young David conversed with his father after killing the giant Goliath, the Bible says "the soul of Jonathan was knit to the soul of David, and Jonathan loved him as his own soul" (1 Samuel 18:1). From that time on, the two men formed a fiercely loyal friendship that was severely tested more than once. After Saul turned against David and even tried to kill him, Jonathan remained loyal and did what he could to keep his friend safe. At one especially critical moment, "Jonathan went to David at Horesh and helped him find strength in God" (NIV).

Do you have friends who can help you find strength in God, especially when your circumstances get dangerous, difficult, or nasty? David had Jonathan; who do you have?

This would be a good place to give a word of caution. The Lord had placed David in Saul's life to encourage him, but Saul's jealousy caused him to eye David with suspicion. The very person God had placed in Saul's life, who in all likelihood would have become the best friend he ever knew, became his number one enemy. The very person God placed in Saul's life to love and care for him was the one that Saul ultimately sought to destroy through manipulation and even murder. Isn't it amazing that we can be so undiscerning and not recognize a friend when God sends him? Perhaps we ought to pray not only for more friends, but that God would give us clarity and discernment to recognize our true friends, the people who genuinely care for us.

I know beyond all doubt that Odus and Viola (who preferred to be called Punk) Scruggs cared for me. Odus knew of my disadvantaged background, including my lack of clothes, books, and my inability to pay for my college education. He knew I constantly depended on some type of help. He and his wife had no living children; their twin boys had both died from kidney disease at the age of two. They told me and Janet that they used to pray at least one of their toddlers would grow up to be a pastor. By then in their late seventies, they knew their dream would never come true. Therefore, Odus told us that one of their passionate desires in life was for God to allow them to "parent a pastor." So they asked us: "Would you two allow us to adopt you?" Their request shocked us, to say the least. As we began to discuss what this would look like, they said, "You are like family to us," and we were. We were constantly at their home, eating together, or going out or shopping or doing something else together. We visited and gave them the opportunity to love on our young children, which they did masterfully.

Eventually they said to us, "We want to buy your clothes, give you spending money, and pay for your education." To say that I felt taken aback would be the understatement of the millennium. They became like second parents to us, two of the best friends we have ever known.

Every two weeks for the next three years, three months, and three weeks, without exception, Odus would give me at least forty dollars in cash after church on Sunday. Who knows how many meals we ate in their home or at a restaurant? He bought me some of the nicest suits I ever owned, with ties and shirts to match. He bought me my first pair of Florsheim shoes and my first pair of genuine Hush Puppies. You do not forget these small details! I can still see some of the nice outfits my children wore, and the pretty dresses my wife wore. You could tell the Scruggs had the gift of giving because they never expected anything in return. They just did it joyfully.

I had the privilege of doing Odus's funeral, and even though I could not be present for his wife's funeral, my wife attended, and I later wrote a long eulogy to honor that precious servant of God. Before Odus died, I visited him at the hospital in the ICU. When he awakened and saw me at the foot of his bed, he became somewhat agitated and seemed to be reaching for something behind him on his backside. He could not speak because of all the tubes in his mouth and nose. After a few moments, however, I realized he was trying to do what he always did when he saw me at church—reach for his billfold to give me a gift.

Odus died the way he lived, as a good friend. He was a giver, not a taker, and I count him as one of the most generous men I have ever known. I thank God for my friend Odus Scruggs.

Take a moment to think through your list of close friends. This may be the perfect day to draft a letter or an email, send a text or a gift, or make a call to let that friend know the difference he has made in your life.

WHAT'S A REAL FRIEND?

If we are not careful, we may forget what a real friend is. We may confuse a genuine friend with a mere acquaintance. Here's an acrostic I use to help me to remember what a real friend looks like.

F—A real friend is someone who becomes like *family*. It took me and Janet years to find men and women who would become as close to us (and often times closer) than our blood kin. But wow, was it worthwhile!

R—A friend is highly *relational*. This relationship is deep, abiding, caring, and compassionate.

I—Friends develop real *intimacy*. When a close friend asks, "How are you doing?" and you don't tell him the exact truth, he will see through your answer and will ask a follow-up question: "No, how are you *really* doing?"

E—A friend is an *encourager*. Paul told his friend Philemon that "the hearts of the saints have been refreshed by you, brother" (verse 7). The word translated "refreshed" means "to blow on." It speaks of a weary army enjoying some much-needed rest. All of us can think of friends who feel to us like a breath of fresh air.

N—Friends are *near* when you need them. They might not always be immediately available, but they will make themselves available at the earliest moment possible.

D—Only *death* separates true friends. I recently lost a dear friend of more than forty years. Dr. Freddy Gage was an evangelist in the Southern Baptist Convention whom God chose to use greatly. Freddy chose to be a dear friend, even referring to me as his fifth son. To this day, even though he is in heaven, I continue to pray for his sons and his wife, Barbara. Our friends don't always outlive us; but even when they depart, they leave a part of themselves inside of us. For the rest of our lives, we move forward with more courage, more conviction, and more genuine love than we ever would have known had we never met these giants among men and counted them as our dear, close friends.

This acrostic prompts me to ask you two questions: First, do you have the kinds of F-R-I-E-N-Ds you need? And second, to whom are *you* going to be that kind of friend?

BEST OF FRIENDS

One of my favorite pictures of friendship in the Bible is that of the apostle Paul and his young mentee, Timothy. Paul referred to Timothy as "a true son in the faith" (1 Timothy 1:2), and on one occasion the apostle called him "man of God" (1 Timothy 6:11). Can you imagine what it must have meant for young Timothy to hear a spiritual hero like the apostle Paul call him a "man of God"?

In his second letter to Timothy, Paul made a series of incredible statements about their friendship (2 Timothy 1:2-6). If you plan to serve the Lord for your entire life, you will need the four characteristics Paul displayed toward Timothy, which I refer to as "expressions of encouragement that fuel enthusiasm." All of us need encouragement. It takes encouragement to stay enthusiastic about the work God has called you to do. And whatever that work is, your heavenly Father will place, in your life, friends who help you to stay engaged.

Paul Loved Timothy

First, Paul *loved* Timothy. When he called Timothy his "beloved son" (2 Timothy 1:2), he used the Greek term *agape*, the strongest word for "love" in the ancient Greek language. In the New Testament, it usually refers to the self-sacrificing love of Almighty God. Paul could not possibly have loved Timothy more.

One of my lifetime heroes, James Dobson, several years ago gave an amazing testimony at a NASCAR event after he had recovered from a massive heart attack. My wife dearly loves NASCAR, and when we went to the NASCAR chapel that day, we heard Dr. Dobson say that two things stood out to him after his near-death experience: He knew who he loved, and he knew who loved him. I believe that is a great statement of friendship.

Paul Prayed for Timothy

Second, Paul faithfully *prayed* for Timothy. He told him, "Without ceasing I remember you in my prayers night and day" (2 Timothy 1:3-4). The Bible teaches that the Lord Jesus Christ ever lives to intercede for His family (see Hebrews 7:25), and nothing is better than to be on the prayer list of the Lord Jesus! But I doubt it would be a bad second to land on the prayer list of the apostle Paul.

One day as I walked through the airport in Atlanta, I thought I recognized, in the distance, a gentleman who was approaching me. Sure enough, it was none other than a hero of mine, Dr. Henry Blackaby. As he drew closer, he called out, "How is the man doing that the Lord instructed me to pray for every day?" What a tremendous blessing to know that I am on this dear man's prayer list! He wrote the bestselling book *Experiencing God*, which greatly influenced my life.

Paul Believed in Timothy

Third, Paul *believed* in his friend Timothy. Every man needs someone to love him, to pray for him, and to believe in him. Paul wrote to Timothy, "I call to remembrance the genuine faith that is in you, which dwelt first in your grandmother Lois and your mother Eunice, and I am persuaded is in you also" (2 Timothy 1:5). Paul called Timothy's faith "genuine." He was saying to his young friend, "I believe in you, Timothy, because you are real. You are genuine, the real deal."

God called me to preach out of a family of poverty. I was a high school dropout who finished his high school education only after studying in the evenings at Cape Fear Technical Institute. I prepared myself for the GED and finally passed on my third attempt.

My pastor, Eugene Gibson, then took me and Janet on a road trip to Gardner-Webb College. He recommended that they give us an opportunity to attend, although I did not have the money and certainly did not qualify for a scholarship. I will be forever indebted to Eugene, the man who preached the night of January 7, 1973, when I was converted. Only heaven will reveal the friend he and his wife, Marian, were to me. I will love them forever.

The Lord worked things out for us to enroll at Gardner-Webb, but we did not know how long we could stay or whether I could make the necessary grades. Even so, within just a few months, I was invited to do some pulpit supply work at Lavonia Baptist Church. After three months, a miracle occurred: In July 1976, the church asked me to become their pastor. And so I began on the path that led me to where I still serve today. A friend who believed in me started me on that path.

Paul Helped Timothy

Fourth, friends *help* us. Paul wrote to Timothy, "I remind you to stir up the gift of God which is in you through the laying on of my hands" (2 Timothy 1:6). Paul desired to see Timothy passionate about Christ and His work. The word picture about "stirring" up the gift of God refers to a flame in danger of going out or burning very low. Paul wanted to remind Timothy that although only God can place a man in ministry, he wanted to help fan Timothy's flame into full blaze. The apostle was saying to him, "I tell you this to encourage you and to let you know that I love you, I pray for you, I believe in you, and I desire to help you."

Sometimes the best help a friend can give is to provide some encouragement. Years ago when I accepted an invitation to speak in the chapel service of Mid-America Baptist Theological Seminary in Memphis, Tennessee, I felt very afraid. I had never spoken in a theological institution at a seminary level. The night before I was to preach, I stayed with a friend, Donald Pope, who was a student at Mid-America. I slept very little that night. I felt tense and more than a little anxious about standing before professors, faculty, the president, and the student body to preach the Word—even though the president, Gray Allison, and his brother, Phil, had already greeted me warmly and made me feel welcome.

The morning I was to preach, I believed I had God's message for the school. Just before I got up to speak, Dr. Allison introduced me to one of his faculty, Dr. Roy Beaman. I had never heard of Dr. Beaman, but when Dr. Allison introduced him, he said he used to teach Greek at New Orleans Baptist Theological Seminary, where he had taught

Adrian Rogers and Dr. Allison himself. I thought, *Wow, this man knows the language; he has been around a long time. I had better be careful what words I speak from the Greek text and how I translate them.* To say this put a little extra fear in me is a vast understatement.

During my sermon, I felt a peace and confidence from the Holy Spirit. Afterward, I was asked to remain available to talk with students and faculty. All were kind and encouraging, which gave me a sense of relief, but at one point when I looked up, I saw Dr. Beaman at the back of the line. I thought, *Oh my, what is this dear man of God going to say to me?*

I needn't have worried. He told me that of all the messages he had ever heard, mine from that morning would rank in the top three. By that time, Dr. Beaman was probably around eighty years of age. Only God knows how his encouraging words lifted me. I was in my early thirties at the time, and I probably needed to hear his words more than he needed to say them. He helped me to have a little more confidence in how I handled the Word of God and proclaimed its truth. That morning, Dr. Beaman became a real friend to me. That is what real friends do: They mark you and God uses them to melt and mold something in you that fills your heart with gratitude and thanksgiving.

All of us need friends who love us, pray for us, believe in us, and help us. May God send someone your way today to fan into full flame your spark of passion!

A PERSONAL BOUQUET

My goal in this chapter is simple: I want to exhort you to find and develop more male friends, or at least deepen the friendships you already have. Rather than give you a list of reasons why you should do this, I want to share what some of my friends have meant to me. I can't mention all of them, but I want you to see how indispensable friends are in every man's life. So here I would like to lay a bouquet to all of my friends, whether I mention them or not.

To John, a man who cuts to the chase. He chooses his words carefully, and you can always count on him to be spot-on honest with you.

For years he met with me weekly as an accountability partner, and to this day, I know he is only a phone call away.

To Morgan, the first person in my life who said to me, "If you ever need to talk to someone about something that may even be dark, something that you wouldn't want anyone else to know, I promise to be your friend, to hear your heart, and to speak truth into your life." For the last thirty years, every week with few exceptions, I get either a text or an email from him. Morgan has always been there for me.

To Buddy, a man God has used to let me know that it is okay to have feet made of clay, and that none of us is perfect. I have always felt so loved and accepted by Buddy and his family.

To Michael, a man who has made himself available to me and who has put his life on hold in so many ways in order to serve me. What a generous friend! I am eternally grateful for this man of God.

To Fred, a fellow pastor and brother in ministry. Through the years, our family has vacationed with him. We have preached for each other, we text each other every week, he calls consistently, we always enjoy our meals together. This is not a high-maintenance relationship; if we do not see each other for months, we simply pick up where we left off. We have low expectations but a high commitment to loving and caring for each other. He is probably one of the best pastor friends I have ever had.

To Mark, a man who went through a crisis similar to my own depression, and into whose life I was able to speak and help him get the assistance he needed. Through that experience, we have enjoyed vacation after vacation together, good times in his home and mine. He has preached to my church, and I've preached to his. We can share the deepest and darkest secrets of our lives. We have become very close personal friends.

To Greg, a man God supernaturally delivered out of deep sin involving alcohol, drugs, and gambling. He has not looked back and has become an example to many believers. This man has chosen to be a great friend to my entire family, and to me. He seemingly has no ceiling to his generosity. He is always looking for someone with a need. You do not have to go to Greg to make a need known; he seems to operate intuitively, sensing when a person has a need and asking how he can help meet it.

Dennis is another lifelong friend—I think our connection began when I attended his mother's funeral soon after I became pastor at First Baptist Church, Woodstock. Ever since then, we have just clicked. He never leaves my presence without telling me what I have meant to him, or mentioning something I did and what it meant to him. If he does not have opportunity to tell me in person, he leaves a long voicemail, sometimes bringing tears to my eyes. When I moved into my current home twenty-plus years ago, Dennis wanted to come, sweep out my garage, and clean the floor before my cars went in. To my surprise, he also put a special plastic coating over the floor that continues to provide protection from most stains. I am absolutely confident of one thing: that I love Dennis, and that Dennis loves me.

To Mike, my BFF. Over the past twenty years, Mike has been that friend who has stuck closer than a brother. He has been a comfort, an encourager, and more than a friend. I can only pray that my investment in his life has been an encouragement to him as well.

Finally, to evangelist Dr. Junior Hill. My father abandoned our family when I was seven years old, leaving my mother with six children; I am next to the youngest. I am not sure how the abandonment of a father influences a boy, but my heart is full of gratitude for the many believing men God has put in my life, such as Dr. Hill. In one of his books, he referred to me as "my son, Johnny." He has always referred to me as his third child. He texts me regularly. As I write, I received five texts from him, five days in a row, with words of encouragement. Dr. Hill just turned eighty-one years of age and continues to preach all over the world—and yet he finds time to speak frequently into my life. Men like Junior Hill give me more courage, more conviction, and more genuine love.

Thank God that in this Christian life, often referred to as a race or even a fight, someone has my back. I am not fighting alone! I have friends who are pulling for me, praying for me, encouraging me, loving me, helping me, and believing in me. The amazing ways these friends have ministered to me prompts me to ask: To whom am *I* going to be this kind of friend? May God make me that type of friend to others!

A SALUTE TO MY BEST FRIEND

Let me wrap up this chapter by sharing about my best friend, Dr. Jim Law. Jim has served as my senior associate for almost twenty-seven years and is well described in the words of Philippians 2:19-24, where Paul again makes reference to Timothy. I would like to use the apostle's words to describe Jim.

Just like Timothy, Jim is an example of a great servant. Paul described Timothy as "like-minded," which means "like-souled" (see verse 20). When Paul needed something done and he could not do it himself, he usually asked Timothy to do it. That is exactly how I feel about Jim.

Close friends share each other's commitments and burdens. A close friend "sincerely care[s] for your state" (verse 20). That means he naturally, genuinely cares; he is real in his approach to let others know that he sincerely desires to meet their needs. When I read those words, it is as though I can see the face of Jim.

Timothy placed Christ before his own interests (verse 21), and when you observe a man for twenty-seven years as your senior associate and know him as a close friend and fellow pastor, you see these things and know them to be true in his life. In contrast to Timothy, Paul wrote of those who "seek their own, not the things which are of Christ" (verse 21). So often Jim has placed his own interests on the back burner. I have watched him for years and have seen his "proven character" (verse 22). What I have seen is not characteristic of a novice or a person young in the faith, but of someone who has been tested, been through the fire, been through difficulty, and yet still sticks closer than a brother.

Paul said that Timothy had "served with me" in the gospel, and that is what Jim has done with me. The Greek word Paul used connotes being surrendered from any personal plans in order to serve another. Jim Law has put whole chapters of his life on hold, or even laid them aside entirely, in order to serve my agenda as I try to follow Christ.

How do you ever say thank you to a friend who chooses to do so much? I will be forever and eternally grateful for the investment, the sacrifice, the compassion, the understanding, the love, the forgiveness, the help, the belief, and the friendship of Jim Law.

Jerry Falwell used to say that if a man dies with five forever friends, he dies wealthy. If I were to die today—and I am drafting these words on the morning of my sixty-fifth birthday, July 17, 2017—I would die a *very* wealthy man. Thank you to *all* my friends.

13

You Need a Coach

You know the guy can coach when the best basketball player on the planet names him as the top coach in the sport's history—and that superstar has never played professionally for the guy.

"I think he's the greatest coach of all time," declared LeBron James about Gregg Popovich, the longtime coach of the NBA's San Antonio Spurs. "You have to be sharp, mentally and physically, when you go against his ball club."

In 2004, after his rookie NBA season, James played for Team USA, for which Popovich served as an assistant coach. But James has spent most of his time observing Popovich from the opposition's side. "To be able to do what he's done… and change with the game [is impressive]," James said. "Pop has been able to adjust every single time and still, for some odd reason, keep those guys under the radar. I don't understand it."[1]

Certainly, Coach Popovich has impressive credentials. He's won five titles with the Spurs, been named NBA coach of the year three times, and is the longest-tenured coach in the league. What makes him so good?

A 2016 article in BusinessInsider.com claims Popovich "could be the greatest coach the NBA has seen" and says the coach insists that "being honest and holding people accountable" tends to bring the best results.[2] But listen to Popovich himself:

> I think you have to have accountability. For us, the thing
> that works best is total, brutal, between-the-eyes honesty.

I never try to trick a player or manipulate them, tell them something that I'm going to have to change next week.

If it's Tim Duncan and it's a timeout and I don't think he's doing what he should be doing, I'll ask him, 'Are you gonna rebound tonight? Are you gonna rebound at all? Or are you just gonna walk up and down and then we're gonna go to dinner? What are we gonna do?' And he'll listen and then he'll walk back out on the court and say, 'Hey Pop, thanks for the motivation.'…

I think being honest with people is great. Somebody's doing well—you tell them they did well. But you don't have a different system for Duncan, Parker, and Ginobili than you do for number 12, 13, and 14. And a lot of people are afraid of that. You want the best players to like you for all the reasons. It won't work… You need to have the same standards for everyone.[3]

Popovich emphasizes the importance of character, explaining that it permits him to be totally honest with his players. And despite his reputation as a curmudgeon, a lot of stars around the league have indicated they'd love to play for him.

And why not? If Pop could help you win a championship ring through his coaching, then who wouldn't want to call him *Coach*? If the difference between winning a title and watching someone else win the title comes down to a good coach, then why wouldn't you willingly submit to his direction?

Men in all kinds of life situations see the wisdom of this kind of reasoning, so today a dizzying array of coaches have made themselves available in areas far beyond sports: executive coaches, business coaches, life coaches, performance coaches, skills coaches, career coaches, health and wellness coaches, relationship coaches—you name the interest, there's probably a coach for it.

Why is it, then, that in the most important area of life so few of us men even think about seeking out and working with a good coach?

AN EXAMPLE TO FOLLOW

The simplest biblical definition of an effective coach may be what was written by the apostle Paul, who said, "Follow my example, as I follow the example of Christ" (1 Corinthians 11:1 NIV). Paul knew a lot about coaching to win in the spiritual life, and perhaps his most well-known student was a young man named Timothy.

Paul was the elder, more experienced man to Timothy's younger, less experienced man. Paul saw potential in Timothy—that's what made him willing to invest in Timothy's life. Paul knew he wouldn't be around forever, and he was determined to train up Timothy so that his influence would live on after he was gone.

Paul shared his life experiences with Timothy. He brought the younger man on trips, instructed him, encouraged him, and corrected him. Paul revealed his heart to Timothy and willingly made himself vulnerable. He shared both his strengths and his weaknesses. The pair talked through successes and failures, spoke when necessary and listened a lot, and in general made themselves available to each other.

Over time, they grew so close that Paul referred to Timothy as his "true son" (1 Timothy 1:2) and his "beloved son" (2 Timothy 1:2). Occasionally the apostle sent Timothy on difficult assignments that, for one reason or another, he couldn't tackle himself. At the end of his first letter to his valued protégé, Paul wrote, "O Timothy! Guard what was committed to your trust" (1 Timothy 6:20). And in his second (and so far as we know, final) letter to the young man, the apostle said,

> I thank God, whom I serve with a pure conscience, as my forefathers did, as without ceasing I remember you in my prayers night and day, greatly desiring to see you, being mindful of your tears, that I may be filled with joy…You therefore, my son, be strong in the grace that is in Christ Jesus (2 Timothy 1:3-4; 2:1).

As the sun was setting on his apostolic career and life, Paul longed to see Timothy. He had invested a great deal in this young man, and although he remained his coach, the apostle leaned on him for help and support. Twice toward the end of 2 Timothy Paul urged Timothy to make a personal visit. "Be diligent to come to me quickly," he said. "Do your utmost to come before winter" (4:9, 21).

IMITATE HIS FAITH

A good basketball coach teaches his players how to play the game more effectively. He instructs them, models for them, corrects them, encourages them, and does a lot of his work "on the fly" as various situations come up. If you're Gregg Popovich, everything you do is built on a foundation of honesty and solid character. You tell your players the truth, and you never manipulate them.

Good coaches don't insist that their players imitate their style or way of doing things. Certainly they don't demand that the younger men in their charge mimic their personal habits or lifestyle. A good coach models for his players what he expects, but he also wants his players to be who they are as individuals. He doesn't set out to create clones.

A successful life of faith has a lot in common with a successful athletic career. Paul observed that 2,000 years ago, and so he peppered his letters with references to various sporting events. At one time or another he made reference to boxing, track and field, awards ceremonies, and spectators. And although Paul didn't use the word *coach*, he clearly taught that every man could use an older hand in the faith to help him become the man God means for him to be.

Still, you don't imitate the coach's mannerisms, clothing choices, accent, or taste in cars. Rather, you imitate his faith. Hebrews 13:7 instructs us, "Remember those who rule over you, who have spoken the word of God to you, whose faith follow, considering the outcome of their conduct." A good coach provides a healthy model of Christian conduct, a strong walk of faith, uplifting speech, and a focus on Christ. That's what you follow.

People occasionally ask me, "Johnny, who's your coach? Who's your mentor? Who has affected your life the most?" They're not asking me about the guy to whom I feel closest, but who has had the most impact on my life. And for me, there's no question about the answer.

"Adrian Rogers," I'll say. While he was one of the more outstanding preachers of the twentieth century, I often add, "I've probably never owned more than a dozen of Adrian Rogers's tapes." I loved listening to his sermons, but I loved far more the life I saw him lead. *That* is what most molded and shaped my life and ministry.

MY COACH, ADRIAN ROGERS

All of us have been shaped by those who have gone before us and those who have chosen to spend time with us over crucial months or years. I am confident that I am the man I am today because I had the privilege to count Dr. Adrian Rogers as my coach. Several thoughts come to mind.

Dr. Rogers always made me feel special whenever I was in his presence. It seemed as though he had no one else waiting to see him, and he had nowhere else he needed to be. One time I visited Bellevue Baptist Church, where he pastored, just to sit in the back of the auditorium and observe this man of God. What I saw him do, not just on this occasion but at other times as well, greatly influenced the way I do ministry today.

On that Sunday after the service, I watched him stand down at the front to greet both young and old, visitor and member. I know he had to be managing a hectic schedule, yet you would never know it by the relaxed way he took time for everyone. I've seen other "celebrity pastors" finish their sermon and then have someone else end the service in prayer as they slip out of the auditorium and hop in their car to go home. But not Adrian Rogers. He was a pastor first and a preacher second, and he saw his primary ministry as people.

As a result, through the years I have practiced being one of the last people to leave our worship center. If someone is planning to have lunch with me, I normally tell them that I will not be able to leave immediately after the service, because it is my practice not to leave until I have had the opportunity to speak to and greet every person who desires to meet me. Sometimes I get to share the gospel with someone; at other times someone needs my prayer support or just an encouraging word.

Dr. Rogers also made me truly believe that he wanted to know *me*, to know who *I* was. Whenever I got to hang around him, I usually asked to know more about how he became the man of God that he was or what he had done to help Bellevue Baptist Church explode in both evangelism and missions. He never dismissed my questions, but he always turned the conversation around to find out more about me. Inevitably I would leave thinking that what I had *actually* learned from him was that he really cared for others and genuinely wanted to know all about them. He seemed to want to know everything about my church, which at that time was running about ninety people for Sunday morning worship. As I described to him the small things I was doing to try to make a difference, he paid me one compliment after another.

On one occasion, Dr. Rogers asked me to come to his office to visit with him personally. His secretary, Linda, greeted me, and I figured I would be one of many to be invited back to see him. I soon discovered that I was his only guest that day. Once more, as we sat there together, he peppered me with questions. He began to speak to me about the dreams and aspirations I had for my church at the time, Long Leaf Baptist Church in Wilmington, North Carolina, the church where I had come to faith in Jesus.

After I described to him my dreams and aspirations, he asked me to kneel on the carpet in front of him, and then he laid his hands on my head and prayed that God would give me all the desires of my heart that were pleasing to Him. He even prayed specific prayers of request. Janet and I needed a money miracle at the time, and he asked God to send people who were gracious, generous, and capable to help fund the work that God had placed upon my heart.

As I've said, many would consider Dr. Rogers the greatest preacher produced by the Southern Baptist Convention in the twentieth century. He always was well prepared and therefore always had much to say. By his example and exhortation, he taught me to be well-prepared to preach. I often have thought that the sermons I preach on Sunday may not be the best, but they will be the best prepared I know how to do. I pray that I will never have to apologize for the messages I preach because I will have given them my best in my study and preparation time. That's due to my coach, Adrian Rogers.

I once heard Dr. Rogers say, "Be kind to young preachers on your way up, you will have to pass them on your way down." He said this with a chuckle and it still makes me smile, but his observation was correct! I got to know many promising young preachers when they were just starting out, and now that I've been a pastor for forty years, I look around me and so many of these young preachers have turned into great men of God. I so love and admire them all and feel so loved by them, I'm glad that I took the time to care for them and coach them. For this, I must give credit where credit is due and lay a bouquet at the feet of my friend in heaven, Dr. Adrian Rogers. I watched him model this truth.

Many pastors no doubt would say that it was the preaching of Adrian Rogers that influenced them the most. But as I've said, I can say without a shadow of a doubt that I was influenced more by observing his life than by his sermons. While his sermons greatly inspired, informed, and often convicted me, it was his life that God used to help shape me.

I especially appreciate what Dr. Rogers said in one of his sermons, in a moment of brokenness: "A lot of you think I am something special, but if you knew me the way Jesus knows me, you would not be nearly as impressed." Those words are no less true about me, and serve as a constant reminder that it is God who has made me what I am today, and I can take no credit whatsoever.

I remain grateful for the transparency, vulnerability, and honesty of Adrian Rogers. He even taught me how to walk slowly among people. By nature, my tendency is to rush from one place to the next around our church campus. But because of the example of Dr. Rogers, I get up early in the morning and pray that God would help me to pace myself. I have trained myself to walk the halls slowly, look people in the eyes, greet them, and take time to be with them if they need to speak with me. This practice led me to write a statement a few years ago that said, "Ministry is everywhere God may use me. I might do more ministry in the hall or on the way to the pulpit than I will do in the pulpit that day, simply by personally touching someone's life." People matter more than sermons or timetables—I learned that by watching Dr. Rogers.

One day at a convention I was standing outside the main hall when I noticed Adrian Rogers and two other well-known men walking by. Nearby were three young pastors who undoubtedly had hopes of getting their Bible signed, or a handwritten word of encouragement or a Bible verse inscribed in the flyleaf of their Bible. The young men called out to Dr. Rogers and the other two gentlemen by name. The other two men waved, gave a nondescript general greeting, then moved quickly away. Not Dr. Rogers. He stopped and acted as though he had nothing else to do, nowhere else to be, and that no one was more important than these three young preachers. I watched him pull a pen from his jacket and take the time to sign those Bibles. I observed as he peered into the eyes of each young preacher and spoke words of encouragement to them, as he had often done in my life: "Where are you serving, young man? That's wonderful. Tell me a little bit about your ministry. Is your wife here with you? I'd love to meet her. Let me pray for you before you leave."

When it comes to good coaching, it's not so much what you hear a coach *saying* as it is what you see him *doing*. The big things are more often caught than taught. That's why Dr. Rogers had such a powerful influence.

When I visited Bellevue Baptist Church for Dr. Rogers's funeral service. I arrived at the sanctuary early, sat in the middle near the front, and fixed my eyes on Dr. Rogers's body lying in the open casket. A large, wooden shepherd's staff had been placed nearby. I thought, *He shepherded me well, and he coached me well*. I am sure many others who were present prayed in the same way I did: "Lord, when I die, may some young preacher, some lay person, view me in my casket and think, *This is the man of God who shaped me by the life he lived*."

FIND YOURSELF A COACH

As I consider the enormous impact Dr. Adrian Rogers had on me, here are six things I've learned from years of watching him in action. He...

- loved the people God called him to pastor, and modeled that love well.

- had a unique way of making others feel important and special to him. Everyone who knew him and spent time with him has Adrian Rogers stories!

- taught me to genuinely care for others by giving them my undivided attention, staying focused on them while they speak to me, and speaking to them words of encouragement.

- loved young pastors, demonstrating his love for them everywhere he went, especially at his church, at conventions, and on seminary campuses.

- taught me to be prepared whenever I preach.

- modeled that you teach what you know, but you reproduce who you are.

Good coaching, as I learned it from Adrian Rogers, *demonstrates* the right thing to do even more than it explains what to do. This is why the Bible encourages us to imitate the faith of more mature Christians. It's not their method or giftedness or personality we are to imitate. Rather, it's their *faith*.

How do you know when you've found the man you'd like to be your coach? You know it when you can confidently pray something like this:

> God, I want to be a man who will believe You like he does. I want to be a man who spends time with You as he apparently does, because he seems to ooze with Your love and the presence and power of Jesus. I always leave him feeling encouraged by his godly behavior and blessed by his kind words. I would love to have him as my coach.

Almost certainly you will never get to where you want to be unless you find a coach who has been where you want to go, whose life of faith you see as worthy of imitation.

So look around you. Observe the men of faith who have touched your life in one way or another. Who could serve as your coach? He doesn't need to be a pastor. In fact, it's better if his life circumstances more closely resemble your own.

Identify a possible candidate and ask him out for coffee or invite him to a ballgame. Tell him of your interest, but don't make a big deal of it. Don't approach him with a contract to sign or a list of forty questions with regard to his qualifications. Rather, see whether he has any interest, and try to determine whether a coaching relationship with this person would be a good fit for you.

In particular, remember that coaching relationships take time to develop. Don't be in a rush. And remember, it's not something that should require mountains of time for either of you. But it can definitely make a mountain of difference.

14

You Need
a Colleague

My main spiritual gift is exhortation. Over the years I've been in ministry, I've had to preach a number of sermons that were difficult to give. When the Bible says something that is likely to be hard for listeners to receive, I preach it hard. I pray that I'm loving as I proclaim it, but I don't soften what the Bible says. When Scripture confronts or challenges people, I exhort my listeners likewise. But it's not easy to do this, and it has made me feel uncomfortable at times.

After church, Janet and I usually go out to eat. One day after giving one of these hard sermons, I ordered only water.

"What do you want to eat?" the waitress asked.

"I'm not eating," I replied.

"You're not eating?" Janet asked, sounding a little alarmed. "What's wrong? Why aren't you eating?"

"I'm nauseated from the sermon this morning," I answered.

When we finished with lunch and the time came to go home, I said to Janet, "Don't take me home. Take me back to my office."

"Why do you want to go back to your office?" she asked.

"Because this has so bothered me," I answered.

"What is it?" she probed.

Now remember, by nature I am an encourager. When I'm called to work outside of my area of giftedness, it does a number on me. But do you know what often happens afterward? It happened that evening.

When I arrived at church that night, a man came up to me and said, "I want to tell you, God flat used you in my life this morning. You encouraged me."

After I got over the shock, how do you think those words made me feel at that moment? When I arrived that evening, I felt worn out, discouraged, deflated. Then a man who had been encouraged by my strong words that morning (although for the life of me, I can't imagine how) came up to me to say how encouraged he was. *I* was the one who needed encouragement that day, and at that moment, he gave it to me. At that instant, he became Barnabas to me.

A SON OF ENCOURAGEMENT

You probably already know that the name *Barnabas* means "son of encouragement" in Hebrew. Barnabas's birth name was actually Joseph. He got the nickname Barnabas from the apostles because of the way he constantly went around encouraging his fellow believers (see Acts 4:36).

As the early church grew and expanded, the apostles heard that God was bringing many people to faith in Antioch, and they sent Barnabas to investigate. "When he came and had seen the grace of God," the Bible says, "he was glad, and encouraged them all that with purpose of heart they should continue with the Lord. For he was a good man, full of the Holy Spirit and of faith. And a great many people were added to the Lord" (Acts 11:23-24).

As a man full of both the Holy Spirit and of faith, Barnabas came by his encouragement naturally. Luke tells us that Barnabas "was glad" when he saw the great work God was doing in Antioch, but I can guarantee you that the new Christians there felt equally glad to host him in their city.

Before Paul (also named Saul) became a Christian, he was a dangerous man zealous to destroy the church. He threw Christians in jail and assisted men who murdered them; he certainly didn't look for ways to evangelize anyone. But after Paul became saved, he tried to join the church in Jerusalem to see how he could use his considerable gifts to serve the Lord. But none of the believers would go near him. "They were all afraid of him, and did not believe that he was a disciple" (Acts 9:26). Given Paul's past, you can understand their hesitancy and fear.

But one man wasn't afraid. "Barnabas took him and brought him to the apostles. And he declared to them how he had seen the Lord on the road, and that He had spoken to him, and how he had preached boldly at Damascus in the name of Jesus. So he was with them at Jerusalem, coming in and going out" (Acts 9:27-28).

Paul, of course, did not come in and go out among the members of the church at Jerusalem without Barnabas leading the way. Without Barnabas, then, there might have been no Paul.

A little later, when Paul's vigorous preaching won him some death threats from Greek-speaking Jews, the church sent him away, first to Caesarea and then to his hometown of Tarsus (Acts 9:30). After that, we don't hear anything about Paul for a while. No doubt he continued to actively tell others about new life in Jesus, but the Bible tells us nothing about his activities during this time.

Quite a while later, when the apostles sent Barnabas to Antioch to investigate the good reports they'd heard about the spread of the gospel, Barnabas realized he needed a helper to go with him. What did he do? He made a beeline for Tarsus to find Paul and bring him back to Antioch with him.

The two men made a powerful team. Initially they were known as "Barnabas and Saul" (Acts 13:2, 7). Barnabas was mentioned first, as if he were the leader. But in the middle of a missionary trip, Luke called them "Paul and Barnabas" (Acts 13:43). Apparently Paul had matured with the help of his encouraging friend and colleague, Barnabas, and from then on, the amazing ministry career of the apostle Paul shifted into high gear.

Would any of that have happened without Barnabas? Maybe, but the historical fact is that God used Barnabas to gift to the church with the man we know as the apostle Paul.

Every man needs a Barnabas in his life—I do, and so do you. Who do you go to when you need to share a burden, admit to failure, talk over some worry, or float a trial balloon regarding one of your ideas to see whether it's brilliant or crazy? Who will love and respect you, but also tell you the truth without flinching?

"Faithful are the wounds of a friend," the Bible says, "but the kisses of an enemy are deceitful" (Proverbs 27:6). You need someone who will not tell you only what you want to hear, but who will speak honestly and yet encouragingly into your life.

James strongly urges us to find a friend to whom we can admit our faults and seek help and encouragement when we need it (see James 5:16). We are to admit our wrongdoing to a faithful colleague who will pray for us and see us through in God's healing process. Not only is confession good for the soul, it is good for our Christian walk.

So let me ask again: Who is your Barnabas? A Barnabas is someone who loves you and yet is honest with you. He will know when to encourage you, and when to challenge you. You need a Barnabas to whom you can be accountable.

No doubt our wives are often great when it comes to encouraging us. They care about us, and they're also willing to tell us the truth in a loving way.

But sometimes you need such words to come from another man. I don't know that I can completely explain this; I just know that is the case. Certain kinds of rebukes and encouragements seem to carry more weight, more gravitas, when we hear them from a strong male colleague.

For example, consider the critical situation described in Galatians 2:11. There, Paul tells us what happened when Peter came to Antioch but failed to live up to the truth of the gospel. "I withstood him to his face," Paul wrote, "because he was to be blamed." I'll guarantee you that Paul loved and admired Peter, but he was not so impressed with Peter that he couldn't rebuke him when it was necessary. I imagine Peter's wife could have said something similar to her husband, but I'm guessing that when this rebuke came from Paul, it carried more weight.

Do you have a Barnabas in your life? If not, where can you find one? We all need a Barnabas in our circle of friends and colleagues—or even better, several of them.

LOOKING FOR BALANCE

I have already introduced you to my Barnabas, but I must give credit where it is due. When it comes to unpacking the difficult things in my life, I know I can turn to Jim Law. He helps to bring such great balance to my perspective.

When I go to see Jim about a pressing situation, he might tell me, "Let me think about that." Then later he will send me a long, detailed email that lists the pros and cons with regard to how I could respond or take action. Without fail, he always offers his support and gives ideas about how to approach a matter in the best way possible, or at the best time possible.

There is a sense in which my wife is a Barnabas as well. She will speak straightforwardly to me without beating around the bush, seeing through the fog to speak clearly into my life. Many times I have sat with Janet and described to her something that bothered me, and she has responded with words of wisdom, instruction, encouragement, and admonition in how to move forward.

Through both Jim and Janet, God has brought great encouragement to me. Jim has the gift of administration, along with many other excellent qualities. Janet is gifted in other ways. Both of them balance me out well and give me different perspectives that help me to land in a good place. I have never felt uneasy about sharing my weaknesses or failings with Janet or Jim. I know that by the time I am finished talking with either one of them, I will have lots to think about and plenty of encouragement to help me make the right decision.

Frequently, however, I am in need of a man's perspective on some situation. And Jim provides that.

How wonderful it is to get someone else's perspective when we are blindsided by a matter that causes deep worry in our soul! In Galatians 6:2, we are told to "bear one another's burdens." Jim and Janet have been incredible burden-bearers for me. Not only will they listen when I tell them what worries me, but they offer great insight. I am grateful that they care enough to reflect upon my situation, pray, and seek the mind of God so that they might share His wisdom with me and help me to meet the challenge I'm facing.

FROM VISION TO REALITY

I am a visionary person, and thankfully, God has surrounded me with men and women who are willing to take my visions, enhance them, and help them become reality. These colleagues often become the hands and feet that help me bring into the real world that which my eyes have seen and my mind has imagined.

There are times, however, when I present ideas that aren't so great, and Jim—or someone else—will be honest with me or bring balance to my thinking.

I'm fortunate to have more than one Barnabas-type figures in my life. And I would be remiss if I did not mention another member of my "Barnabas clan," Dan Dorner. I cannot count how many times I have made arrangements to see Dan when I was wrestling with something that troubled my soul. One time I started toying with an idea that I thought might provide some significant benefits for my family. I thought, *Maybe I should cash in a good bit of my retirement and become debt-free.* When I went to Dan and shared what I was thinking, it would have been so easy for him to give a quick yes or no. Instead, he said, "Let me think that through and develop my response. I'll get back to you." Dan is one of the most methodical thinkers I have ever known.

He came back to me a couple days later, sending me an email that outlined his primary talking points. He began by celebrating my thoughts and telling me why my idea might be a good one. But then he said, "However," and subsequently laid out about ten reasons why he doubted I should proceed. Based on his careful counsel, I did not move ahead.

How easy it would have been for Dan to simply reply, "What a ludicrous plan," or "What a great idea!" Instead, he took the time to look at the matter from several different angles. I still recall reading through Dan's outline and thinking, *Wow, why didn't I come up with any of this?* What a man of wisdom, and what a loving friend!

God places people in our lives who are much wiser in certain areas than we are, and He sends them to us so they can give us counsel, lift our spirits, and provide encouragement when we need it. Where would

I be today had God not surrounded me through the years with colleagues from the Clan of Barnabas?

When I think of those who comprise my "Barnabas clan," I think of individuals who have a clear and unique perspective different from my own. They have an ability to truly *see*. One beatitude teaches us, "Blessed are the pure in heart, for they shall see God" (Matthew 5:8). God speaks into our lives through people who see clearly the things that we don't see—things that they use to help and encourage us.

A Barnabas can see not only where a problem starts, but how it might unfold and how it might end. He can see it from different angles you won't have yet considered.

Often I have tunnel vision when I'm trying to think through some challenge. Countless times I've thought long and hard about how to deal with a critical issue when Dan Dorner has spoken up to give me his thoughts—and it completely changed my plan. Time and again I've wondered afterward, *Why didn't I think of that?* When others have asked me what I thought about Dan's counsel, I often have found myself saying, "I have only one problem with it: I wish I'd thought of it."

Encouragers also care about the men they encourage. You may have heard the saying, "People don't care how much you know until they know how much you care." You need at least one Barnabas in your life who will care for you and who will tell you the truth in love.

Every Barnabas I know is thoughtful. Even after I have received the advice or encouragement, long afterward he will email me or leave thoughtful voicemails or send texts as he prays through my challenge until I make a final decision.

Finally, encouragers often play the role of "enlargers." They help you to grow bigger, stronger, and more useful for the kingdom of God. They enlarge you. They help to accomplish in your life what Isaiah the prophet talked about so long ago:

> Enlarge the place of your tent, and let the curtains of your
> habitations be stretched out; do not hold back; lengthen
> your cords and strengthen your stakes. For you will spread
> abroad to the right and to the left, and your offspring will

possess the nations and will people the desolate cities. Fear not, for you will not be ashamed; be not confounded, for you will not be disgraced; for you will forget the shame of your youth, and the reproach of your widowhood you will remember no more. For your Maker is your husband, the Lord of hosts is his name; and the Holy One of Israel is your Redeemer, the God of the whole earth he is called (Isaiah 54:2-5 ESV).

I have no doubt that every member of the Clan of Barnabas will one day have this word chiseled permanently on his tombstone: *Others*. These friends continually think about how they can use their influence, wisdom, skills, experience, knowledge, and understanding to help others.

So once more: Who fills the critical role of Barnabas in your life? Who do you know that you can go to when you need a listening ear, a fresh perspective, an encouraging word, faithful counsel, or an honest opinion? Who will love you enough to tell you the truth, but do so in a way that builds you up and gives you renewed courage to face your challenges?

THEY STAY EVEN WHEN THEY GO

Two chapters ago I mentioned my friend Freddy Gage, an evangelist who went to be with the Lord not long ago. I guess a good way to speak of Freddy is to say that when he departed to heaven, he left a part of himself in me.

I will never forget the sound of Freddy's voice. When I think of something he said to me, I can hear him as though he were still here with me. I can remember moments with Freddy when he made me feel amazingly special and greatly encouraged me. He was a valued friend.

Freddy called me often, and the year before he died, he chose to come to Atlanta to spend Father's Day with me. He came to church with Janet and me, and had lunch at our home. I will never forget that day. Freddy Gage was a card-carrying member of the Clan of Barnabas.

My mind leaps next to another true friend and priceless colleague, Homer Lindsay, the former pastor of First Baptist Church in Jacksonville, Florida. He invited me to preach at his annual Bible Conference, one of the largest in Southern Baptist circles. The night I preached, he had to go to the hospital; he died a few days later.

It was Homer who taught me, "If you know what you have and you like it, be reluctant to leave it." That wise statement has helped to keep me at First Baptist Church Woodstock, where I'm now in my thirty-first year of ministry. Homer would say, "It takes four to five years to become the pastor," and in my ministry of training up young ministers, I have quoted his statement countless times.

How grateful to God I am for such wonderful colleagues who have so greatly influenced and positively affected my life! The Clan of Barnabas has diminished here on earth because some of these people have departed for heaven, but I have fun imagining what their reunions must be like when they see each other again.

Who plays the role of a Barnabas in your life? Which male friends can you call on who will gladly offer to do for you what Freddy Gage, Dan Dorner, Jim Law, and others have done and continue to do for me?

I don't want you merely to think of who these people are or might be. I want you to write down their names. On the lines below, write the names of a few men in your life who belong to the Clan of Barnabas. To the right of their names, describe how they encourage, challenge, help, and equip you to keep moving ahead as you face challenges.

Then write each of these men a note and mail it to them, expressing your gratitude for what they have done for you and your delight in your friendship. Members of the Clan of Barnabas are wonderful at encouragement, but all of them could use some encouragement of their own. Why don't you give it to them?

15

YOU NEED A COLT

It takes a lot more than talent to make it in the National Football
League. Legion are the guys with scary talent who either wash out
of the NFL or who never even make the roster of one of the league's
thirty-two teams. Why is that?

One big reason is that many of these talented athletes lack a mentor,
someone who can show them the ropes, help them navigate the many
pitfalls en route to stardom and give them the kind of veteran wisdom
they so desperately need. With that in mind, the NFL Players Association created a mentor program staffed by former pro players and tar-
geting young men at risk, even those still in high school. The program

> was developed by players, for players, to help student ath-
> letes reach their academic, intellectual and athletic potential
> in order to fulfill aspirations of playing intercollegiate athlet-
> ics. With the focus of developing skills both on and off the
> field, our former NFL players will draw from personal expe-
> riences in order to guide, teach and support student-athletes
> towards the goal of receiving an athletic scholarship.[1]

I'm glad that the program has broader aspirations than just helping kids win athletic scholarships. The NFLPA says the strength of the
program "lies in the desire of the Mentors to 'reach down and teach up'
the next generation of football players who dream of earning a college
scholarship, getting a degree, and playing at the ultimate level of the
National Football League."[2]

Does it work? It appears to, at least for many gifted young athletes. Austin Kendall, a four-star high school recruit who chose Oklahoma University over Auburn, Clemson, Tennessee, and others, said,

> The NFLPA Mentor Program has been an awesome resource during my journey through high school. It's nice to have someone you can talk to other than your parents and coach that can offer guidance. After my sophomore year I struggled with the decision to transfer back to my original high school. Coach Brunell and I talked about it and he made me understand that I needed to do what was best for me and my family. He also reminded me to think about more than football during the recruiting process. He told me I needed to look at schools I would attend even if I wasn't playing football.[3]

After I wrote those last few paragraphs, I reread them, and several terms and phrases jumped out at me:

- Reach their potential
- Fulfill aspirations
- Draw from personal experiences
- Guide, teach, and support
- Reach down and teach up
- Nice to have someone you can talk to
- Offer guidance
- Made me understand
- Think about more than football

The retired players who serve in the program—including Mark Brunell, a nineteen-year veteran at quarterback who mentored young Austin—don't *have* to do what they do. They choose to serve because they want to leave a lasting, positive mark on the game outside of the playing field. As they say, they want to "reach down and teach up."

What would you say if I suggested that God is asking *you* to do the same thing?

WHERE ARE THE MENTORS?

I've already suggested that every Christian man, including you, needs a coach and a colleague. But now I want to say that to become the fully mature man God calls you to be, you also need to learn how to build into the lives of other men. You need to become a mentor, in other words. And every mentor needs a young colt to train.

I explained in chapter 13 why I see Paul's mentorship of young Timothy as a great model for us all. Paul himself described both the nature of his mentoring and its importance when he told Timothy, "You therefore, my son, be strong in the grace that is in Christ Jesus. And the things that you have heard from me among many witnesses, commit these to faithful men who will be able to teach others also" (2 Timothy 2:1-2). Paul's instruction here seems to anticipate, by many centuries, the terms and phrases listed a moment ago: "reach their potential," "fulfill aspirations," "draw from personal experiences," "guide, teach and support," "reach down and teach up," "offer guidance," "made me understand." Paul knew nothing of football, but he knew a lot about mentoring, and the principles of the latter don't change much over the years.

But if that is so, then why don't we see more Christian men accepting the challenge to mentor younger men in the faith? Why aren't more of us bringing younger men along? Why aren't more of us sharing with others what God is doing in our lives? If I had to name the key reason, I think I could put it in one word: *selfishness*. Too many of us are out to get instead of give.

Jesus said we ought to exist for others. We ought to have a heart that says, "God, what can I do to add value to other men instead of just looking for what's in it for me?"

The Bible says, "Let nothing be done through selfish ambition or conceit, but in lowliness of mind let each esteem others better than himself. Let each of you look out not only for his own interests, but also for the interests of others" (Philippians 2:3-4). This passage explains why the apostle Paul decided to "reach down and teach up" a young man named Timothy. Paul invested his life in this young man who had lots of potential. He chose to affirm and encourage him, to instruct, guide, equip, and help bring him to maturity. In other words, he became Timothy's mentor.

A lot is being said these days about win-win situations and defining a winner, so I came up with my own definition: A winner is a person who helps others win. In the business world, a winner is usually seen as someone who works to get ahead so everybody can admire him and attend his seminars and hear how he did it. But I believe a real winner is a man who equips other men to win. Nothing brings greater joy to my life than watching God generate real disciples through the ministry He's given me.

There is a great little secret hidden in the roll call of faith in Hebrews 11. The chapter lists name after name of great men and women of God, and it says about Abel, "Through his faith, though he died, he still speaks" (verse 4 ESV). My hope is that after I pass off the scene, because of my commitment to training up younger men to serve Jesus, my influence will continue for decades to come. That's why I am committed to mentoring.

Who are you mentoring? What are you doing today that will guarantee your impact for Jesus Christ in the next generation?

WHAT IS MENTORING?

Mentoring is a process in which a more mature man chooses to get involved in the life of a less mature man in order to help him grow into the godly man God wants him to be. It's not about a program, a curriculum, or a rigid training system. It's all about relationship.

I once sat around a table with forty-three leading pastors, some of the sharpest minds in ministry. Jimmy Draper asked me to take my mentoring material and share it with the others. A man spoke up from across the table and said, "That's what I want to do. I want to have a mentoring school. Brother Johnny, can you get us a mailing list of guys?"

"Fellas," I said, "you've all missed it. The main ingredient in mentoring is relationships." Mentoring isn't just saying, "Come join my program." It's about relationships, and relationships take time. They also can be inconvenient.

To show people I care, I try to return all my phone calls. I know 're are a lot of pastors who don't do that. I might see one of them at a conference and, in front of a group of people, he will say, "Johnny Hunt doesn't have a better friend in the whole world. I love him with all my heart." And I will think, *I haven't been able to get him to return any of my phone calls.* True friendship and true mentoring both require showing a lot of personal concern—and that can be inconvenient.

Again, mentoring is a *relationship* that God allows us to establish with other men in order to spur mutual spiritual growth. The colts you mentor will also help *you* to grow and learn. If you want your colts to grow, then you need to continue growing yourself. I also desire to reach my God-given potential, whatever that is. Since my potential is not limited unless God is limited, that creates a lot of excitement in my heart.

As long as you live, you learn, and as long as you learn, you live. If you stop learning and growing today, you will stop being effective tomorrow. The effectiveness of my ministry as a pastor depends on my continuing to grow; that's the only way I can keep the people in my church growing.

IN THE DAILY-NESS OF LIFE

Most real mentoring gets done in everyday living rather than in classroom settings. I didn't even know I was mentoring others until people began to say, "You're my mentor." I thought, *I am? Well, what am I doing?*

One time I traveled to Conover, North Carolina, to speak for a couple of nights at the church of a good friend. I went alone, and while at my overnight accommodations, I heard a knock at the door. I thought, *Who could that be?* The time hadn't come yet for the pastor to pick me up. When I opened the door, there stood a young preacher. "I called your secretary," he said, "and she told me you would be over here preaching for a couple of days. I was able to get away, so I jumped on a flight and came over. I'd like to stay with you."

"Well, come on in," I said.

He walked in and took the second bed. A little later, I heard another knock at the door. And then a third. By the time all the knocking had ended, five young preachers had shown up, all of them unannounced.

We had two double beds, we got some rollaway beds, and all five of them spent the next couple days with me.

I didn't sit down with them and say, "Okay, guys. It's Sunday school time. Open your Bibles." No, we sat around and one guy would say, "I'm struggling in this area." Because I had struggled with similar issues earlier in my ministry, I said, "Let's talk about it." We moved from issue to issue like that—no set curriculum, just whatever life brought up.

Mentoring happens in the hurly-burly of everyday living. It's the time you spend with other men in a car, at a ball game, in the aisles of the hardware store. You can do that, can't you?

A MINISTRY OF MULTIPLICATION

Mentoring is a ministry of multiplication. I am greatly encouraged when I watch how God multiplies the work of young pastors I've mentored.

One week I addressed sixty pastors in our association on world evangelization, exhorting them about how they could get personally involved. When I returned to my office, the foreign mission board sent in fourteen personnel. Later we had 100 pastors from America and Canada come in. Then I turned right around and enlisted twelve of the leading pastors in America to go to Hong Kong with me to visit unreached people groups and see how they could personalize missions ministry in their own church.

All of that kindled a fire in me. I thought, *I've been involved in the lives of 172 preachers and never left home this week!* Through my interactions with them I had the potential of touching many more thousands of other people—without leaving home. That's the power of mentoring.

It's not necessary for you to be a pastor to experience the multiplying effect of mentoring. Each life you touch goes on to touch several other lives, perhaps dozens. You never mentor a solitary man; you always influence all the men and women in his life. And sometimes the flame you kindle in one person will grow into a wildfire affecting hundreds. How can that not encourage you?

Spiritual encouragement fuels enthusiasm in your life. The reason many men no longer seem enthusiastic about their walk with God is that it's been far too long since they received a good dose of encouragement. Remember, every time you build into the life of another man, you launch a process that ideally will never end. If you touch Steve's life and Steve touches someone else's life, and that person does the same… where does it end?

WHAT IT TAKES

What does mentoring require on the part of the mentor? What must a mentor be prepared to give? You must be able to commit to these four goals:

1. Spiritual Commitment

You have to stop playing games when it comes to your responsibilities as a Christian. You must make a firm spiritual commitment to make a real investment in the lives of other men.

It's not easy returning all of the many calls I get, but I am committed to doing so. I schedule blocks of time. I tell my assistant, "I'll be on the phone for the next two hours, returning calls." I also read all my mail and answer the questions asked of me. That gets tough, instead of having someone reading it and answering it all for me. But I have made a spiritual commitment to those who look to me for guidance. I want to be involved in their lives. I want to help.

2. A Commitment to Life Change

The older I get, the more I'm committed to building disciples, as opposed to merely counting how many people come to Christ. Too often the measure of a church's success is how many people get saved, while not enough emphasis is placed on building believers to spiritual maturity.

When I meet with other pastors, the conversations are usually about last Sunday's decisions rather than about making disciples. If you *really* want to know what happened in my church last Sunday, you'll need to call me in about a year. What really counts is not how many people signed decision cards on Sunday, but how many of them are still around after a year. I want "fruit that remains," the kind of sticky decisions that change lives forever. I want to know about those who are still around, still growing, and multiplying and making a difference.

I'm on the lookout for young guys who follow the example of Heidi, a young aerobics instructor in our church. She made an impression on me just six weeks after she got saved. Every week, she introduced another person to Jesus. She was bouncing off the walls. I'd call her high-energy saved. Right after she became a Christian, we had a missions conference. She'd never heard of missions. She approached me immediately and said, "Pastor, I want in on missions. I'll go anywhere in the world."

Around that time I met a guy in the hallway and asked him, "How are you doing?"

"I'm doing fine," he said. "My name is John. I'm thirty-two years old, I've been a devout Catholic all my life, but my sister Heidi led me to Jesus last week."

Heidi couldn't sit still. That's fruit that remains, and it's still producing. I'm committed to life change and seeing disciples produce fruit to the glory of God. I think we could do with more men bouncing off the walls.

3. A Commitment to Excellence and High Moral Values

The late Howard Hendricks said, "High on [the] priority list [of a mentor] is the development in another individual of excellence, so that the individual grows in his Christian life to hate the mania of mediocrity, the attitude that anything is good enough for God."[4]

To be a mentor means to give the best you have. You should treat your young colt like a prince. Give him a valuable chunk of your time, not just your leftovers. Make a costly investment in him. Do your best. You want to be your best for Jesus and do your best for the man you're mentoring. Whatever you do, try to do it with excellence. Avoid the mania of mediocrity like the plague that it is.

4. A Commitment to Objectives

Clear-cut objectives are measurable. You can look at what you're trying to accomplish and say, "God is at work here." The devil will try to beat you up and say, "Why are you wasting your time? You can't make any real difference. It may look like it, but it's just a mirage." When he says that, take him back to the cross, where he can't follow you all the way. Point to the measurable objectives you set out at the beginning, then remind him of the victories God is bringing to your young colt through the clear-cut objectives you've set.

WHAT DOES MENTORING DO?

My experience tells me that mentoring accomplishes at least seven great results in the lives of the men you mentor.

1. Mentoring Develops a Man

When you mentor someone, you're saying to him, "I want to see you reach your maximum potential for Jesus Christ." It's the same principle Paul shared with the church at Colossae when he said he would warn every man and teach every man "with all wisdom, so that we may present everyone fully mature in Christ" (Colossians 1:28 NIV). The word translated "mature" can also be rendered "perfect." Paul continued, "To this end I also labor, striving according to His working which works in me mightily" (verse 29). An effective, God-honoring mentor puts a distaste in the mouth of his young colt for the mania of mediocrity. Instead, that colt begins to say, "I want to do my best for the kingdom of God."

We just *have* to kick it into a higher gear in order to reach the world for Jesus Christ!

About 7.5 *billion* people are alive on this planet today. All but about 25 percent of them have had a chance to hear the gospel. Earlier in my life I used to say that only half the world had heard; now, three-fourths have heard. It is an attainable goal that every person in the world will soon have the opportunity to hear the gospel of Jesus Christ. I find that incredible. What a way to mentor and develop a man—to get him involved in reaching people for Jesus!

2. Mentoring Gives Clear-Cut Priorities

What do you want to have achieved by the end of your days? And what price are you willing to pay for it? The success of your life will be determined only at its end.

Many years ago, as I started my twentieth year of pastoring, my church gave me a six-week sabbatical. A lot of guys might think, *Man, that sounds great, to be off for six weeks!* But I've been working since I was fifteen and pastoring since I was twenty-three. I'd never been off of work for more than ten days at a time. After about two weeks, I felt miserable. I didn't know what to do with myself. Instead of twiddling my thumbs, I was eager to get back to work.

But I'd made a commitment that during my sabbatical I wouldn't preach anywhere. I had to rest, be with my family, kick back, and just cool it. My deacons wanted me to return refreshed. I'd call preachers and say, "I plan to worship with you on Sunday night. I'd like to take your family to dinner."

"Great," they'd say, "then preach for me."

That almost killed me! I wanted to shout, "Yes!" but I had to say, "I can't." I didn't preach a single sermon for forty-two days. Until that time, for almost every week since I had become a pastor, I'd preached two or three times each week.

Eventually I fell into a state of deep discouragement. I'd go for two- and three-hour walks. I felt embarrassed. I didn't recognize the unsettling feelings and emotions I was experiencing and I found myself asking questions like, *What if my ministry were over?* and *What have I accomplished?* The question that bothered me the most, however, was this: *What have I been trying to accomplish?*

If you haven't carefully defined what you want to accomplish, then how can you possibly measure your success (or lack of it)? How can you have clear-cut objectives if you're not even sure what you're attempting to do?

There must come a time when you power down long enough to say, "What, exactly, am I attempting to do? What do I hope to accomplish with my life?" If you can't answer those questions, then how are you going to lead anyone else, including your colt, to a good destination?

What clear-cut objectives do you have for the man or men you mentor? What precisely do you want to accomplish? If you don't know, then spend some time looking inside yourself and ask, "Lord Jesus, what am I all about? What am I doing here? What do You want me to accomplish with this mentoring relationship?"

In my own life, I've found that sometimes I need to eliminate in order to concentrate. Could it be that if you pulled away for a few days, spent time fasting and praying, and asked God to speak to your heart and show you His agenda for your life, that you might be able to let go of some of your commitments so you can be more committed to what God has for you?

3. Mentoring Builds Leaders for Tomorrow

I'm a product of men making significant investments in my life. And life is too short for me to make mistakes as I figure out what God would have me to do, when other men have already made those mistakes. By listening to my mentors, I can save myself a lot of heartache and avoid making poor decisions.

That's what you're doing as a mentor. You're helping your colt avoid some of the dead ends and roadblocks you've had to overcome. He'll commit enough mistakes on his own, so help him to detour around the ones you've had to deal with.

4. Mentoring Gives a Sense of Accomplishment

When I'm mentoring younger men, I never feel that I'm just spinning my wheels. Sometimes my mentoring takes me away from my church and I'll call the office to see if I had any messages. A number of times the response has been, "You've had a lot of calls, but no messages."

"Really?" I'll say.

"Yes, because when we tell them where you are and who you're with, they rejoice and say, 'Praise God. That's important and this can wait; I'll call him back next week.'" In other words, when people know that I'm mentoring some young colts, helping them become the men God calls them to be, they are thrilled because they know that's a good thing. The work of mentoring gives me a great sense of accomplishment, which often spreads to others.

5. Mentoring Builds Deep Relationships

I am not into first impressions. I realize that sometimes, a first impression may be the only one we have the opportunity to make. Still, if we were to get to know each other, I would hope that you'd respect me more after spending some time with me. Good speakers may generate a lot of fans, but good mentors generate deep respect.

There are some men who, at one time or another, were my heroes... until I got to know them personally. Then I didn't respect them nearly so much. Don't let that be true about you as a mentor. The more that other men get to know you, the more they should be able to say, "I see incredible integrity there. This man genuinely cares for me." That kind of respectful relationship takes time to develop.

I'm in an accountability group right now in which I've built some deep relationships with a few great guys. My encouragement is that you develop deep relationships with a few choice men, not superficial interactions. That's how you can be sure you'll make a lasting impact.

6. Mentoring Holds You Personally Accountable

Healthy accountability becomes a major deterrent to evil, and I need all the deterrents I can get. I don't want to break God's heart. I don't want to break my wife's heart, or the hearts of my children, my staff, my peers, or of all the younger ministers God has placed in my life. Being a mentor holds you personally accountable to your colts. They look to you for leadership, to guide them and help them navigate tricky waters. They're *there*, and you need to be there for them. Mentoring gives you a sense of belonging and being needed, and that, in turn, helps you to realize just how accountable you are.

7. Mentoring Strengthens You Personally

The Bible says that one man can put 1,000 to flight, and two men can put 10,000 to flight (see Deuteronomy 32:30). Isn't that amazing? I wonder why it doesn't say that two men can put 2,000 to flight instead of 10,000? The point is that together, we can have a greater impact. We can accomplish more. Wouldn't that make you feel great? Paul put it well when he wrote that his children in the faith were his greatest joy (see 1 Thessalonians 2:19). In the same way, your colts become your greatest joy. Together, you can do much.

When I watch how God blesses the young men I've mentored, it thrills my heart. Mentoring—and seeing the results—gives you the opportunity to rejoice as God works in the lives of other men. Seeing other men grow will both strengthen and encourage you.

THE POTENTIAL OF MENTORING

How do you find the promising young colts who need a mentor? How do you identify the men who are worth the investment of your time and counsel? Here are three simple suggestions:

1. *Pray that God will bring some good candidates into your life.* Ask, "God, who is it out there? Who could use an older hand like mine in his life to help him become all that You want him to be?"

2. *Look for those who are committed.* Try to identify those who look to have potential, those who are serious about their walk with Jesus. Make sure they're hungry for spiritual growth.

3. *Look for men who are teachable.* If a man won't listen, he's unteachable. This quality's a nonnegotiable. Look past the veneer and make sure the man has a teachable spirit.

If you're earnest about being a mentor and you commit the matter to God, He will send you someone. You can count on it.

FOR LACK OF A MENTOR

A few years back, a ton of NFL scouts had their eyes on a wildly talented young athlete whose name was Colt. The kid was "insanely" gifted—that's the word a lot of newspaper articles used. A video posted on YouTube showed he was able to jump right out of a swimming pool from a depth of three or four feet. How does anyone even *do* that?

Adults who knew the young man universally described him as a "good kid," but always mentioned his tough home life. He got a scholarship to play football for a national powerhouse and as a freshman showed glimmers on the field of his enormous potential. But then things went south.

He quit the team after his sophomore year, hoping to catch on with an NFL team, but before any of that could happen he got busted for drug use. And then he began a steep downward spiral. Court appearances. Convictions. Jail time. Expressions of remorse and, "I'll do better."

In June 2017, an article in his home state newspaper said he'd been "sentenced to 30 more days in jail for corrections center escape."[5] The judge encouraged Colt to get "clean and sober" and declared, "You're really on the edge of both life and the legal system." Another criminal conviction, the judge said, would likely lead to a prison sentence.

I wonder: What might have happened in this young man's life had an older man, a mentor, stepped into the gap? Would we be seeing Colt make crazy, impossible, acrobatic catches in the NFL? Would he be making headlines of a different sort?

We'll never know, because Colt didn't have a mentor.

What young colt in your sphere of influence needs a mentor? As a man seeking after Christ, why couldn't you be the mentor he so urgently requires?

EPILOGUE:

Speaking the Truth Will Set You Free

For more than twenty years, the First Baptist Church of Woodstock has hosted a ministry called The City of Refuge, intended to help those in ministry who are struggling. The struggles vary: A broken marriage, rebellious children, the overwhelming stress that comes with a pastoral calling. Wounded men and women come to us for all sorts of reasons.

I think of one young couple who came to The City of Refuge many years ago. According to the husband, they had come because of his wife's inability to cope with the day-to-day challenges of the ministry. "She's really struggling," he told us. Not long into their time at The City of Refuge, however, we discovered that the real problem went much deeper. In fact, it was the husband, and not the wife, who had the major struggle.

Once this hurting couple got settled in a safe place where they believed they could reveal how they really felt and what was truly going on in their hearts, the reality of their situation slowly began unpeeling, layer after layer. The pastor had *far* deeper and much more sinful issues than his wife. It still amazes me that this husband and wife came to us because the *pastor* desired to get some help for his wife, but in the end, it was mostly about the pastor coming clean.

This man had fallen into pornography, and then from pornography to living it out. He and a woman in his church had gotten sexually involved with one another. His secrecy and his lack of vulnerability and transparency had turned his household into a place of utter turmoil. Yes, the wife struggled with the day-in and day-out challenges of serving the church; but her problem got amplified many times over by the inexplicable situation in her own home. She just couldn't get her arms or mind around it. Once the truth came out, however, everything seemed to become very clear to the wife.

Over the next year and a half, this couple, through transparency and honesty, took their hidden sins and dealt with them. And the Lord did a remarkable work in their lives. While they are no longer in ministry today, we've heard good reports that God has blessed their home, strengthened their marriage, and deepened their relationship. They appear to be living a contented and joyful life together.

How it encourages me to hear of messy situations in which God steps in and makes a huge difference in people's lives! The enemy of our souls wants us to keep silent about the dark secrets we've hidden in forgotten corners. He wants us to stay silent. But as you've seen many times over in this book, truth *always* trumps the lie. It's speaking the truth that will set you free.

I pray that you will trust God with whatever secrets you may be hiding, for I know you will find the Lord faithful. I also pray that you will seek out a mature brother or two with whom you can share your heart. That's the way to once again walk in victory! Choose today to bring the dark things of your life out into the light of His presence and His Word. Become the man God intends for you to be.

May God bless you.

Notes

CHAPTER 1—THE SILENCE OF THE RAMS

1. Gregory L. Jantz, "Brain Differences Between Genders," *Psychology Today*, February 27, 2014, https://www.psychologytoday.com/blog/hope-relationships/201402/brain-differences-between -genders.

2. Jantz, "Brain Differences Between Genders."

3. Jantz, "Brain Differences Between Genders."

4. Jantz, "Brain Differences Between Genders."

CHAPTER 2—BREAK THE CHAINS OF FEAR

1. Peter Allen and Chris Brooke, "'Band of Brothers' American World War Two hero exposed as a fraud," *Daily Mail*, July 10, 2009, http://www.dailymail.co.uk/news/article-1198143/Band -Brothers-American-World-War-2-hero-exposed-fraud.html#ixzz4nDt91QTb.

2. Timothy George, *Faithful Witness: The Life and Mission of William Carey* (Christian History Institute, 1998).

CHAPTER 3—PRIDE: THE ULTIMATE PATH TO SELF-DESTRUCTION

1. C.S. Lewis, *Mere Christianity* (New York: HarperOne, 2015), 123.

2. Lewis, *Mere Christianity*.

3. C.S. Lewis, *Mere Christianity* (New York: Harper Collins, 1952, 2001), 121-22.

4. Lewis, *Mere Christianity*, 124.

5. Lewis, *Mere Christianity*, 127-28.

CHAPTER 4—BRAIN RUTS

1. "Internet pornography by the numbers; a significant threat to society," Webroot, https://www.web root.com/us/en/home/resources/tips/digital-family-life/internet-pornography-by-the-numbers.

2. Mary L. Pulido, "Child Pornography: Basic Facts About a Horrific Crime," Huffpost, January 23, 2014, http://www.huffingtonpost.com/mary-l-pulido-phd/child-pornography-basic -f_b_4094430.html.

3. Penny Starr, "Pornography Use Among Self-Identified Christians Largely Mirrors National Average, Survey Finds," CNS News, August 27, 2015, https://www.cnsnews.com/news/article/ penny-starr/pornography-use-among-self-identified-christians-largely-mirrors-national.

4. Morgan Lee, "Here's How 770 Pastors Describe Their Struggle with Porn," *Christianity Today*, January 26, 2016, http://www.christianitytoday.com/news/2016/january/how-pastors-struggle -porn-phenomenon-josh-mcdowell-barna.html.

5. Terry Cu-Unjieng, "Why 68% of Men in Church Watch Porn," Conquer Series, May 6, 2014, https://conquerseries.com/why-68-percent-of-christian-men-watch-porn/.

6. Cu-Unjieng, "Why 68% of Men in Church Watch Porn."

7. "Brain activity in sex addiction mirrors that of drug addiction," University of Cambridge, July 11, 2014, http://www.cam.ac.uk/research/news/brain-activity-in-sex-addiction-mirrors-that -of-drug-addiction.

8. Ed Stetzer, "Jesus and Sexual Deviants," *Christianity Today*, August 17, 2011, http://www.chris tianitytoday.com/edstetzer/2011/august/jesus-and-sexual-deviants.html.

9. Stetzer, "Jesus and Sexual Deviants."

CHAPTER 5—A WISDOM CALL

1. "14 Warning Signs of a Secret Alcoholic," www.new-hope-recovery.com/center/2013/10/08/14 -warning-signs-of-a-secret-alcoholic.

2. John MacArthur, "Beer, Bohemianism, and True Christian Liberty," August 9, 2011, Grace to You, https://www.gty.org/library/blog/B110809.

3. Statement from Josh Franklin, source unknown.

4. "Youth Exposure to Alcohol Advertising on Television, 2001 to 2007," The Center on Alcohol Marketing and Youth, Executive Summary, June 24, 2008, http://www.camy.org/_docs/ resources/reports/archived-reports/youth-exposure-alcohol-advertising-tv-01-07-full-report.pdf.

5. "Underage Drinking," National Institute on Alcohol Abuse and Alcoholism, January 2006, https://pubs.niaaa.nih.gov/publications/AA67/AA67.htm.

6. "Underage Drinking," National Institute on Alcohol Abuse and Alcoholism, https://pubs.niaaa .nih.gov/publications/underagedrinking/Underage_Fact.pdf.

7. Daniel Akin, "The Case for Alcohol Abstinence," http://www.danielakin.com/wp-content/ uploads/old/Resource_617/The%20Case%20for%20Alcohol%20Abstinence.pdf.

8. Joe Thorn, "Akin on Alcohol," JoeThorn.net, July 1, 2006, http://www.joethorn.net/blog/ 2006/07/01/akin-on-alcohol.

9. Russell Goldman, "Laura Bush Reveals How George W. Stopped Drinking," ABC News, May 4, 2010, http://abcnews.go.com/Politics/laura-bush-reveals-george-stopped-drinking/ story?id=10552148.

10. Bob Stein, "Wine Drinking in New Testament Times," *Christianity Today*, June 20, 1975, 10-11.

11. Stein, "Wine Drinking in New Testament Times."

12. Norman Geisler, "A Christian Perspective on Wine Drinking," *Bibliotheca Sacra*, January-March 1982, 51.

13. Danny Akin, "God's Guidelines for the 'Gray Areas' of Life: Wise Decision-Making in a Wicked World, Part 8," Between the Times, September 8, 2008, http://betweenthetimes.com/index .php/tag/robert-stein/.

14. National Institute on Alcohol Abuse and Alcoholism, "College Drinking," December 2015, https://pubs.niaaa.nih.gov/publications/collegefactsheet/collegefact.htm.

15. National Institute on Alcohol Abuse and Alcoholism, "College Drinking."

16. Adrian Rogers Legacy Collection, "James," https://adrianrogerslibrary.com/wp-content/ uploads/2016/08/James-2016.pdf.

17. The original source where I obtained this information is unknown, but you'll find these statements and similar ones cited on websites relating to alcohol abuse.

18. Ibid.

CHAPTER 6—THE PRESSURE OF PROVIDING

1. "The things that make men feel insecure," *Daily Nation*, September 11, 2015, http://www.nation
   .co.ke/lifestyle/saturday/The-things-that-make-men-feel-insecure/-/1216/2866340/-/ia2f2qz/-/
   index.html.
2. "The things that make men feel insecure."
3. "The things that make men feel insecure."
4. Yuki Noguchi, "Retailers scrambling to adjust to changing consumer habits" http://www.npr
   .org/2017/05/02/526560158/a-rapid-shakeup-for-retailers-as-consumer-habits-change
5. Noguchi, "Retailers scrambling to adjust to changing consumer habits."
6. "Young Chinese couples face pressure from '4-2-1' family structure," August 25, 2010, http://
   en.people.cn/90001/90782/7117246.html.
7. "Young Chinese couples face pressure from '4-2-1' family structure."

CHAPTER 7—I NEED A MONEY MIRACLE

1. OECD. Stat at http://stats.oecd.org/Index.aspx?QueryId=51648.
2. Erin El Issa, "2016 American Household Credit Card Debt Study," nerdwallet, https://www
   .nerdwallet.com/blog/average-credit-card-debt-household/.
3. John Piper, *Desiring God* (Portland, OR: Multnomah, 2003), chapter 7.

CHAPTER 8—MY WIFE TALKS
ENOUGH FOR BOTH OF US

1. *Huffington Post*, "Biological Evidence May Support Idea That Women Talk More Than Men,
   Study Says," http://www.huffingtonpost.com/2013/02/21/women-talk-more-than-men-study
   _n_2734215.html.
2. Claudia Hammond, 12 November 2013, "When it comes to conversation, are women really
   more likely to be bigger talkers than men?" http://www.bbc.com/future/story/20131112-do
   -women-talk-more-than-men.
3. Onnela, Jukka-Pekka, et al., "Using sociometers to quantify social interaction patterns," *Scientific Reports*, 15 July 2014.
4. Onnela, Jukka-Pekka, et al., *Scientific Reports*. 15 July 2014.
5. Steven Stosny, "Marriage Problems: How Communication Techniques Can Make
   Them Worse," *Psychology Today*, February 23, 2010, https://www.psychologytoday.com/
   blog/anger-in-the-age-entitlement/201002/marriage-problems-how-communication-tech
   niques-can-make.
6. Stosny, "Marriage Problems."
7. Stosny, "Marriage Problems."
8. Stosny, "Marriage Problems."
9. Stosny, "Marriage Problems."
10. Stosny, "Marriage Problems."
11. Andrew Murray, *Humility* (Chicago: Fleming H. Revell, 1973), chapter 7.

CHAPTER 10—THERE'S HOPE FOR DEPRESSION

1. Dr. Keith Ablow, "Robin Williams' death: Depression as bad as cancer and as stealthy," Fox News Opinion, August 13, 2014, http://www.foxnews.com/opinion/2014/08/12/robin-williams-what -would-have-told-actor-about-depression.html.

2. Jared C. Wilson, *Gospel Wakefulness* (Wheaton, IL: Crossway, 2011).

3. Ablow, "Robin Williams' death."

4. "11 Facts About Suicide," DoSomething.org, https://www.dosomething.org/us/facts/11-facts -about-suicide.

5. Al Hsu, "When Suicide Strikes in the Body of Christ," *Christianity Today*, April 9, 2013, http:// www.christianitytoday.com/ct/2013/april-web-only/when-suicide-strikes-in-body-of-christ .html.

6. "2012 Suicide Data Report," Department of Veteran Affairs, https://www.va.gov/opa/docs/ Response-and-ExecSum-Suicide-Data-Report-2012-final.pdf.

7. John Ortberg, "Joyful Confidence in God: The Dark Night of the Soul," May 18, 2016, http:// www.faithgateway.com/joyful-confidence-god-dark-night-soul/#.WZNfoGCpXcs.

8. John of the Cross, as cited by Ortberg, "Joyful Confidence in God."

9. John of the Cross, as cited by Ortberg.

10. John of the Cross, as cited by Ortberg.

CHAPTER 11—IN THE TORMENTER'S HAND

1. William Barclay, William Barclay's Daily Study Bible, Matthew 18, https://www.studylight.org/ commentaries/dsb/matthew-18.html.

CHAPTER 13—YOU NEED A COACH

1. Brian Windhorst, "LeBron James says Gregg Popovich is greatest all-time NBA coach," ESPN, January 20, 2017, http://www.espn.com/nba/story/_/id/18515342/cavaliers-lebron -james-says-spurs-gregg-popovich-nba-all-greatest-coach.

2. Scott Davis, "Gregg Popovich has a brilliant philosophy on handling players, and it exemplifies the Spurs' unprecedented run of success," *Business Insider*, March 18, 2016, http://www.business insider.com/gregg-popovich-philosophy-on-handling-players-exemplifies-spurs-success-2016-3.

3. Davis, "Gregg Popovich."

CHAPTER 15—YOU NEED A COLT

1. See at https://www.nflpa.com/mentorprogram.

2. See at https://www.nflpa.com/mentorprogram.

3. Austin Kendall, as cited at https://qa.nflpa.com/mentorprogram.

4. Howard Hendricks, "A Mandate for Mentoring," in *Seven Promises of a Promise Keeper* (Nashville: Thomas Nelson, 1999), 36.

5. http://www.oregonlive.com/hillsboro/index.ssf/2017/06/colt_lyerla_sentenced_to_30_mo.html.

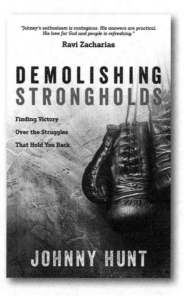

DEMOLISHING STRONGHOLDS

Ever wonder how to be a man of God in the trenches of life—in the day-to-day trials and temptations that hound you? It's not impossible! God's promises and strength are real, and you can claim them today.

Whether you feel beaten down by your past failures or trapped in a corner by your current struggles, let hope lift you up. Pastor Johnny Hunt offers the biblical encouragement and guidance that will help you…

- navigate the dangers and discouragements of daily life
- take practical steps toward taming your negative habits
- use your blessings to influence others for God's glory

It's time to learn how to break spiritual strongholds so you can move forward in God's will and become the kind of man you've always wanted to be.

To learn more about Harvest House books and
to read sample chapters, visit our website:

www.harvesthousepublishers.com

HARVEST HOUSE PUBLISHERS
EUGENE, OREGON